A Dress for Diana

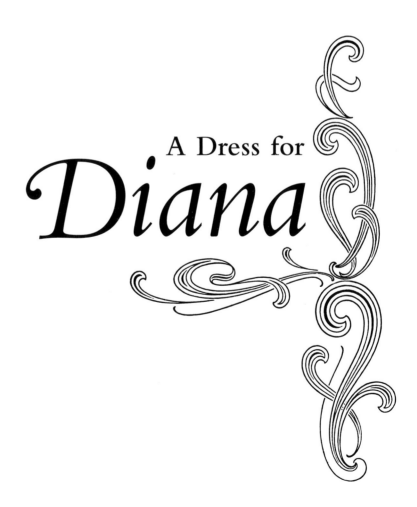

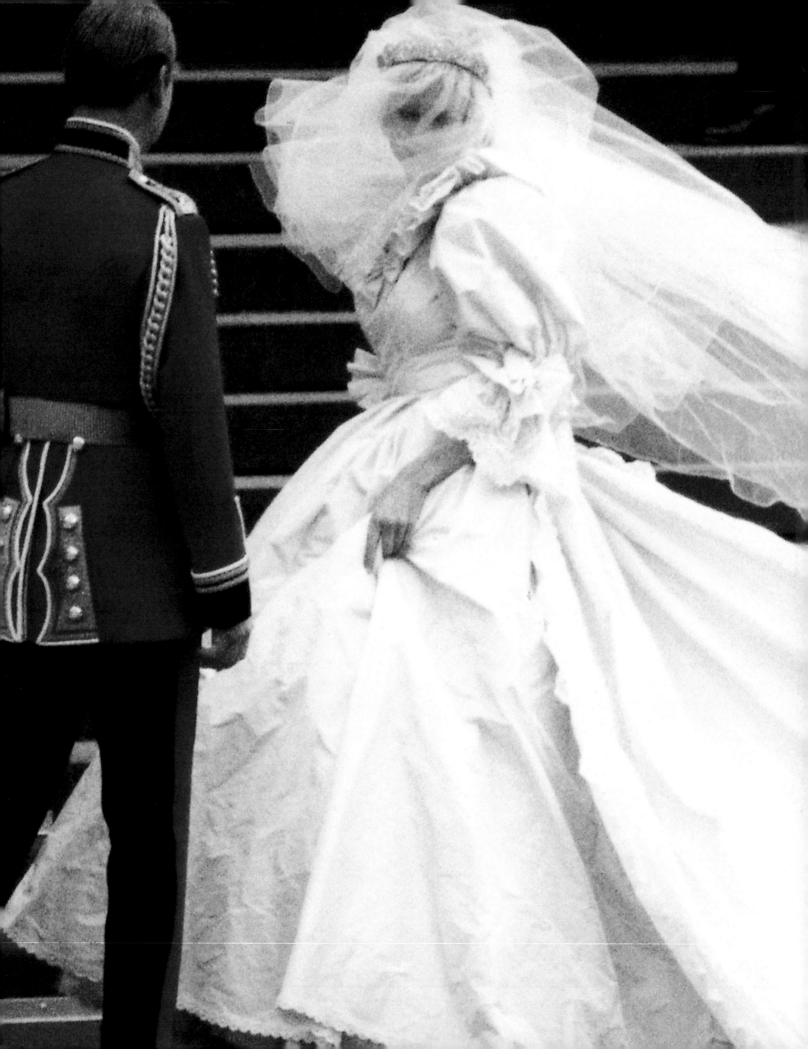

A Dress for
Diana

DAVID EMANUEL &
ELIZABETH EMANUEL

COLLINS | DESIGN

An Imprint of HarperCollinsPublishers

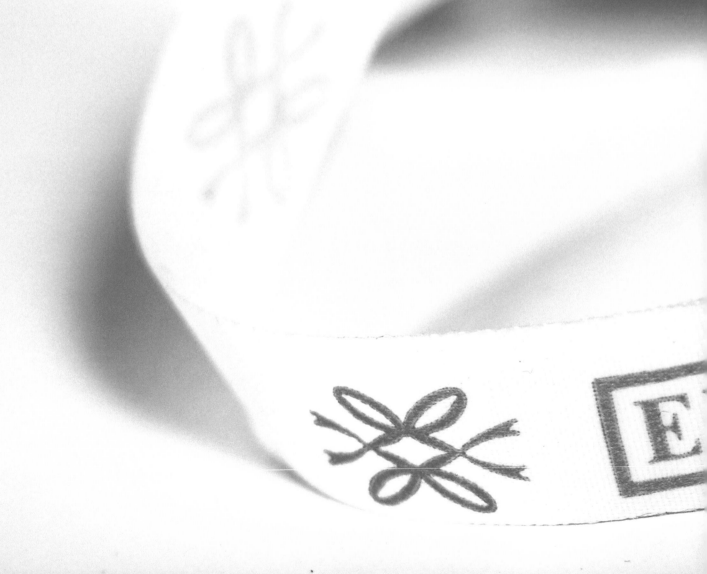

DEDICATIONS

To my wonderful children, Oliver and Eloise, and my entire family in Wales. In remembrance of my brothers Aeron and Ifan ... and loving memories of my amazing mother, Elizabeth.

DAVID EMANUEL

In loving memory of Mom and Dad, whose love and support throughout my career made everything possible.

ELIZABETH EMANUEL

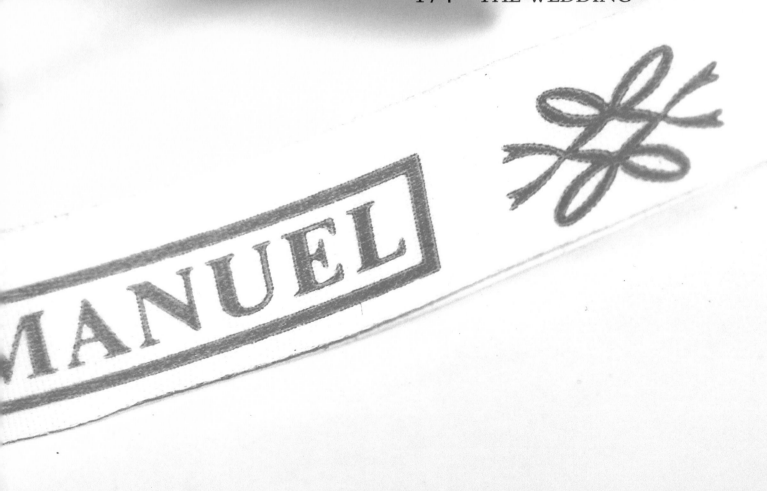

CONTENTS

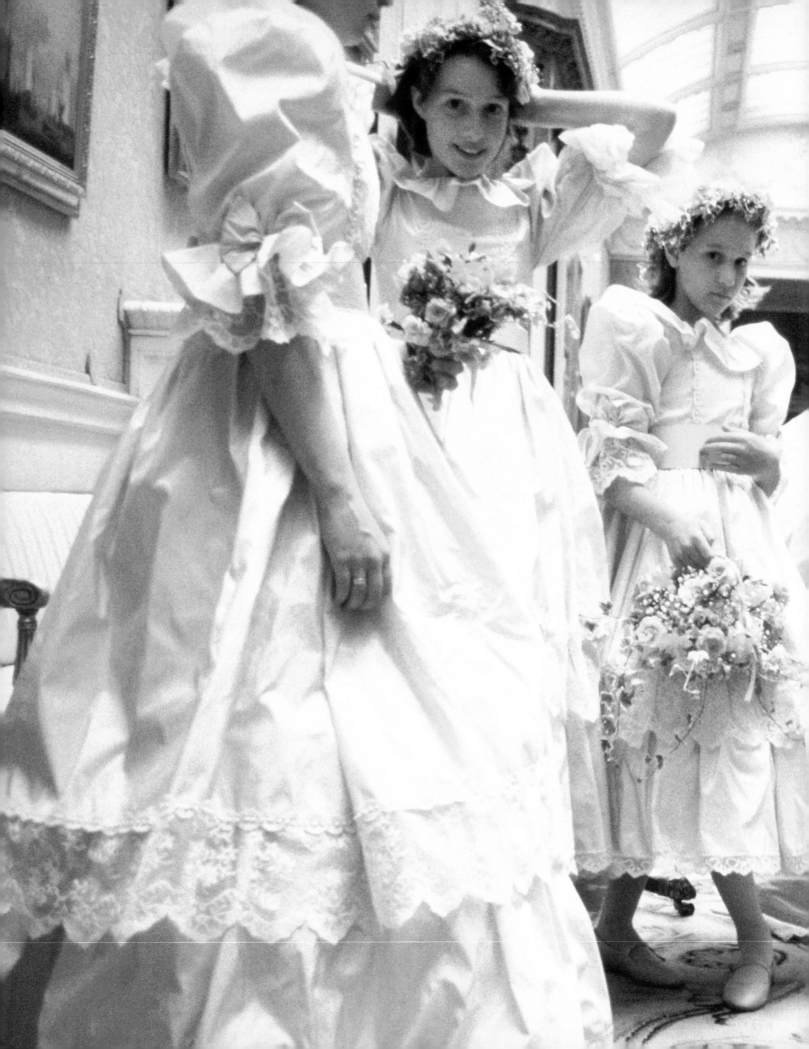

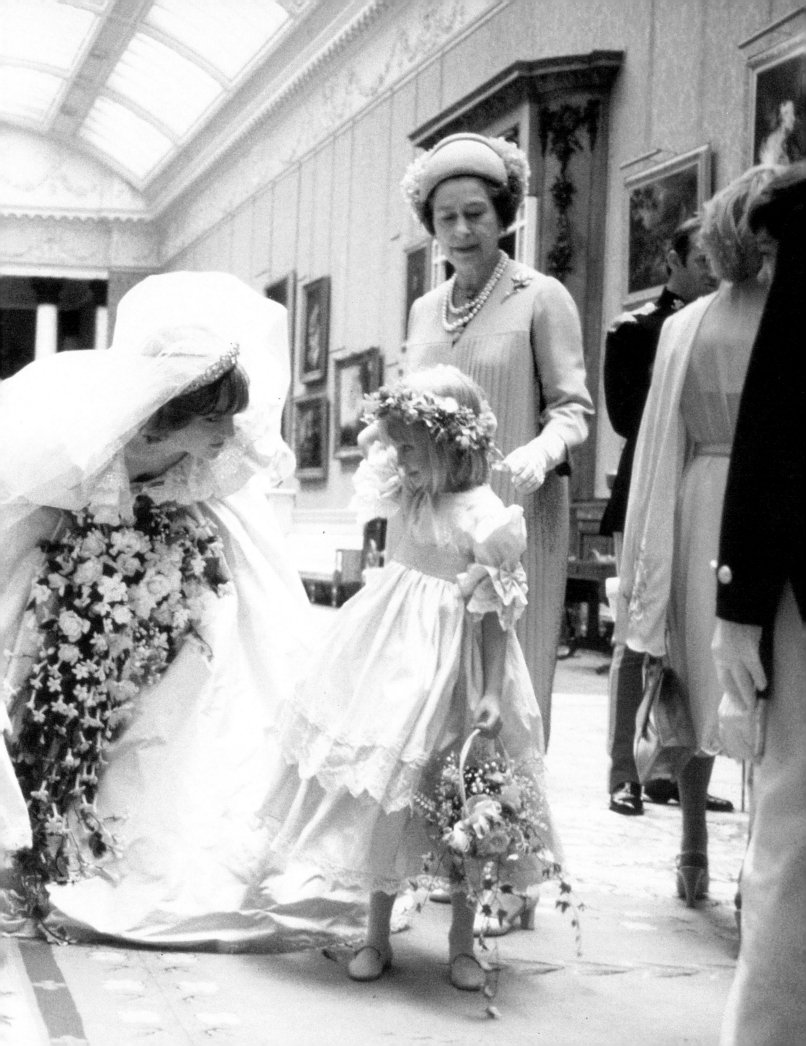

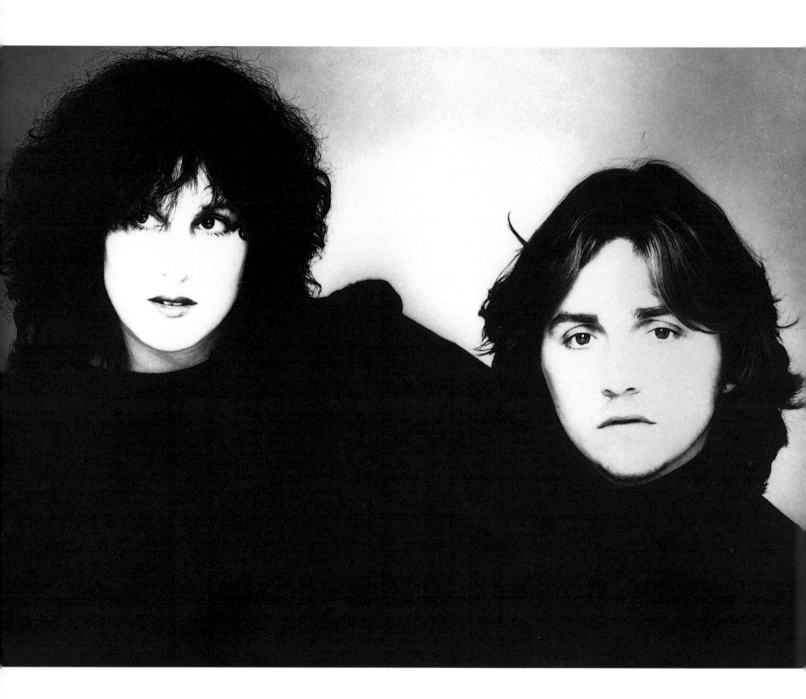

PREFACE

When Diana walked down the aisle on that glorious summer's day in 1981 to marry HRH The Prince of Wales, our duty was done. Every piece of silk taffeta fabric, the dress toiles, paper patterns, sample bodices, antique lace, sketches, letters and every single pearl and sequin were packed in tissue paper and locked away in a series of trunks, which were kept anonyomously in a bank vault deep in the City of London, where they have remained to this day.

It seems hard to believe that twenty-five years have passed since that historic day. It was the most magical day for everyone, from the huge crowds on the streets to the hundreds of millions who watched the event at home on their televisions. But for those of us who were actually involved, it was something that is hard to put into words – it was a day that changed our lives forever. To have witnessed, and even to have played a part, however small, in that "fairytale wedding" was an unbelievable privilege, and one for which we will be eternally grateful.

To mark this twenty-fifth anniversary, we would like to share with you our story, our personal recollections of the roller-coaster months from that first phone call to the Throne Room of Buckingham Palace. This is the story of the biggest commission of our lives – to design the most famous wedding dress of the twentieth century.

And all of this was for a girl called Diana, a lovely, kind-spirited and fun-loving person. This book is in her memory and for all Diana's fans around the world.

DIARY OF EVENTS 1981

JANUARY 8TH	Debra rings for dress needed for Prince Andrew's 21st birthday. Comes in at 2.30PM.
JANUARY 13TH	Liz sends designs to Lady Vestey.
JANUARY 28TH	Blouses go to Felicity Clark at *Vogue*.
MARCH 4TH	M.H. for fitting for wedding dress. Debra calls – "Would you do me the honour...".
MARCH 6TH	Debra comes in for first discussions.
MARCH 9TH	Strapless black dress goes out to Debra for party at Goldsmiths' Hall.
MARCH 10TH	Buckingham Palace announces we are to design the wedding dress.
MARCH 11TH	Debra in at 10.30AM for design meeting.
MARCH 13TH	Meet Stephen Walters re. silk.
MARCH 18TH	Debra in for fitting. Clive Shilton (shoes).
APRIL 8TH	Royal bridesmaids Catherine Cameron and Sarah Jane Gaselee. Debra drives us to Buckingham Palace for first visit. Meet Oliver Everett.
APRIL 16TH	Lady Sarah Armstrong-Jones for measurements.
APRIL 23RD	Jim and Bert (security guards) arrive.
APRIL 24TH	Liz, David, Rose and David Noel to Securicor for identity-card photographs.
APRIL 28TH	Fabric arrives for the dress. Ring St. Paul's to find out width of the aisle. Debra rings with more information re bridesmaids.
APRIL 30TH	Debra comes in with Clementine Hambro. Lots of press at the door.

MAY 9TH	Fitting with Sarah Jane Gaselee.
MAY 20TH	Roger Watson (lace).
MAY 21ST	3.15PM: Debra, Catherine Cameron, Clementine Hambro for fittings.
	5.00PM: Lady Pamela Hicks and India Hicks.
MAY 27TH	Debra and Sarah Jane Gaselee for fittings.
JUNE 19TH	HRH Princess Margaret and Lady Sarah Armstrong-Jones.
JULY 1ST	Debra's birthday.
JULY 21ST	To Buckingham Palace for carriage rehearsals at Royal Mews.
JULY 22ND	11.00AM: final fitting for Debra with Clive and Julie Shilton.
	6.00PM: wedding rehearsal for bridesmaids at St. Paul's.
JULY 24TH	Shocking-pink, silk-taffeta dress delivered to the palace.
JULY 27TH	4.30PM: rehearsal at St. Paul's. 7.00PM: David and Liz to pre-wedding ball at Buckingham Palace.
JULY 28TH	11.00AM: deliver dresses to Clarence House.
JULY 29TH	The wedding day.
	10.00AM: film crew arrives at Brook Street.
JULY 30TH	Collect all materials from Buckingham Palace and Clarence House.
AUGUST 3RD	Wedding dress and bridesmaids dresses to St. James Palace.
AUGUST 4TH	Exhibition at St. James. Liz and Caroline deliver trunks to bank for safekeeping.

NOTE: To maintain total secrecy within our studio, we always referred to Diana as Debra.

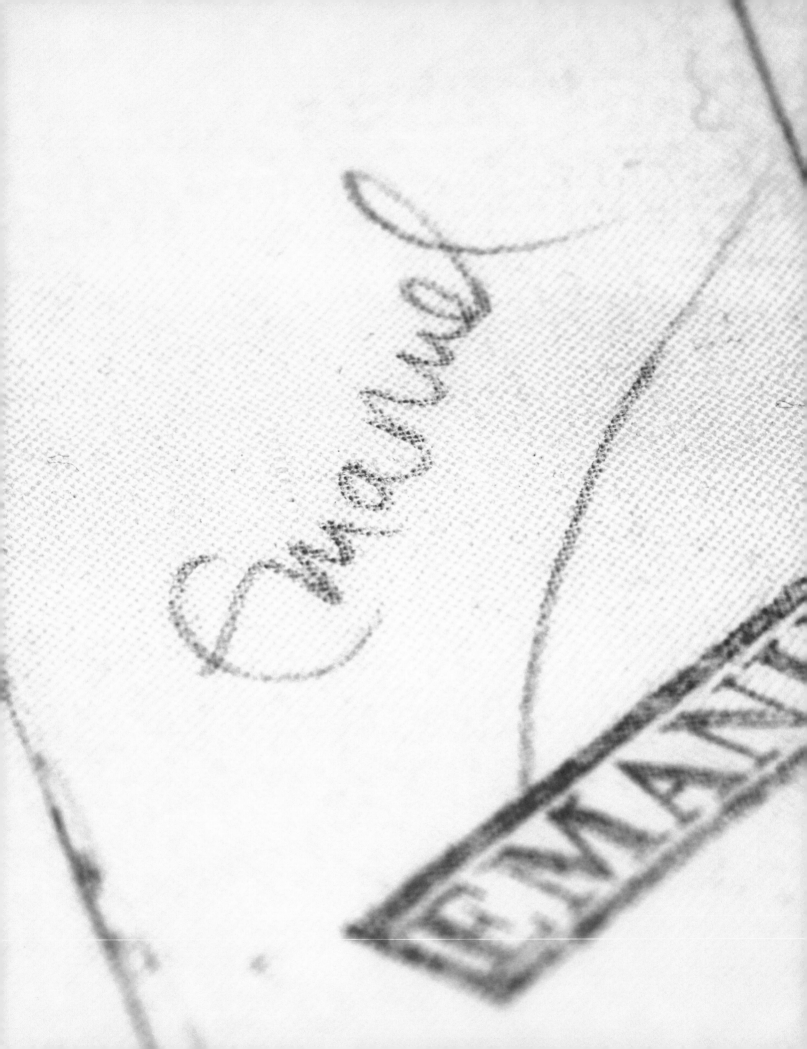

THE EARLY DAYS

On the day of what has come to be seen as *the* Royal Wedding, we were still trying to adjust to the amazing fact that, despite being relative newcomers to the fashion world, we had been chosen by the future Princess of Wales to design her wedding dress. But no-one at that time could have foreseen the extraordinary impact that Diana would make on the world or the influence the dress would have on wedding fashion.

We had graduated from the Royal College of Art in London only four years earlier, having met each other at Harrow School of Art, where we were both already committed to careers in fashion. From the start, we got on very well, partly because we were both so ambitious, dedicated to fashion, but also because we were both determined to study at the RCA. Indeed, we became the first married couple to be accepted into the Royal College of Art.

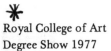

Royal College of Art
Degree Show 1977

School of Fashion Design

23 Cromwell Road, London SW7 2DF
01-584 5020 ext 281

David Emanuel

Fashion Designer

73 Portman Towers
George Street, London W1

01-935 6390

Born in Wales 1952
Cardiff College of Art 1970-73
Harrow School of Art 1973-75
Diploma in Fashion Design 1975

Elizabeth Emanuel

Fashion Designer

73 Portman Towers
George Street, London W1

01-935 6390

Born in London 1953
Harrow School of Art 1971-75
Diploma in Fashion Design 1975

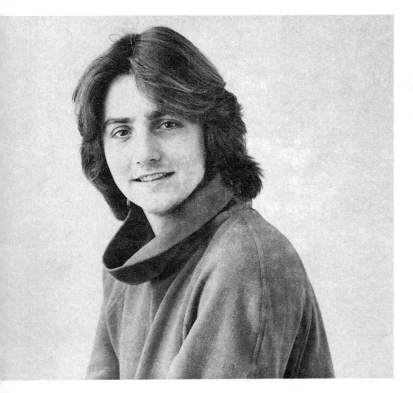
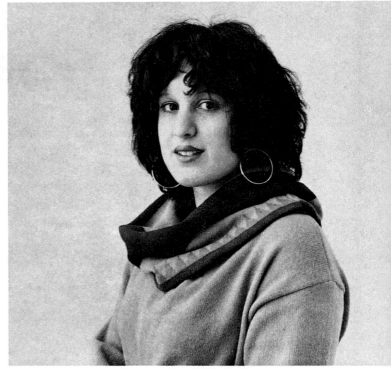

Above Our entries in the Royal College of Art's degree show
catalogue of 1977. We prepared for two years for our final degree
show, and its success helped launch our careers.

The Royal College of Art has an extraordinary reputation: top fashion designers from around the world come to the RCA to pick the best of the crop from each year's graduates to employ in their design studios. We knew that the most important names in the fashion industry would be in the audience for our final degree show.

Over the Christmas holiday before we were due to graduate, we hatched an idea to combine our individual styles to create one double-length collection that would stay in people's minds. David would design daywear and Elizabeth evening wear. To unify the collections, everything would be white. Our professor would not allow this saying that it would be unfair to the other students. Hence we would have to draw our names out of a hat for the show's running order. Fortunately, we picked the last and the penultimate places, so we did get our way in the end!

While we were at college, we had taken a trip to Paris, where Elizabeth came across a stall in a flea market with a fantastic assortment of antique lace, pearls and sequins. She collected masses of vintage textiles to bring back to London and they become the inspiration behind her whole collection and indeed, defined her look, which from then on was characterized by lots of ruffles and lace.

The finale of Elizabeth's collection was a romantic, frothy wedding dress, complete with bridesmaids dresses. We must have managed to seduce the audience with the collection because at the end of the show there were chants of "Emanuel! Emanuel! Emanuel!"

EARLY DAYS
AT BROOK STREET

Our success with our final show at the Royal College of Art resulted in a lot of very positive publicity. Many fashion editors of daily national newspapers and glossy magazines wrote glowing reviews of our work. But our early career was also launched by famous names who had been at the show and who had admired – and, more importantly, talked about – our clothes. Girl- about-town and television personality Lyndall Hobbs bought one of the first dresses we ever designed.

Although we always worked together at college, we had different influences and styles, and it was not an immediately obvious decision for us to create our own fashion label together. As had been witnessed in our show at the RCA, Elizabeth loved anything vintage and romantic, while David was drawn by the elegant. (His greatest style icon was Audrey Hepburn, who, of course, had a wonderful knack of looking breathtakingly beautiful yet natural.) In terms of fashion designers, David adored Valentino's work while Elizabeth favoured the clothes of Dior. But as we were married, and didn't relish the thought of being in different countries – Valentino was based in Rome and Dior in Paris – and as we were already beginning to make a name for ourselves thanks to the show at the RCA, we decided to jump in with all four feet and combine our talents to create the Emanuel look.

We knew it was going to be very risky to start our own business, but we felt we had to take the plunge. We didn't really want to work for anybody else and, anyway, we felt we already had our own very distinctive look. Fortunately, Elizabeth's family agreed to provide us with financial backing and so we began to hunt for suitable premises.

"It was a wonderful beginning and, looking back, it seemed as though everything was going our way. Was fate leading us to receive the commission of a lifetime?"

One day, as we were driving up Brook Street in London's West End, we happened to notice a "To Let" sign up on a little building by Haunch of Venison Yard, near Bond Street. The location was perfect: close to Claridges and with Vogue House, which is in Hanover Square, just a stone's throw away. We guessed it would be too expensive for us to contemplate, but in fact it turned out to be very reasonably priced and – perhaps fortuitously for us – it belonged to Frederick "Freddy" Fox, who was the Queen's milliner. We had no doubts that we had found the new home for our fledgling business. There was a little side door and we put up a brass plaque saying "Emanuel" and we moved into this small space above a florist's. (We shared the same toilet, so we had to get used to trails of leaves and flowers up the stairs.) Almost immediately, we recruited a third member of the team, our machinist, Nina, who quickly became indispensable.

We had planned to turn our final RCA show into the first Emanuel collection. What we hadn't planned on was having all the daywear clothes and patterns stolen from our car while we were out shopping one day. It was all hands to the deck as the three of us worked furiously day and night to remake the stolen collection.

When we first started, we had no telephone – we had to go to the Post Office to make phone calls – but we did have a typewriter, which we used to answer the many letters that we received after *Brides* magazine featured the wedding dress we had designed for our final show at the RCA. And here in our new tiny home in Brook Street, we began to develop our style, our look, all the time concentrating on wonderful fabrics, beautiful cuts and impeccable finishes.

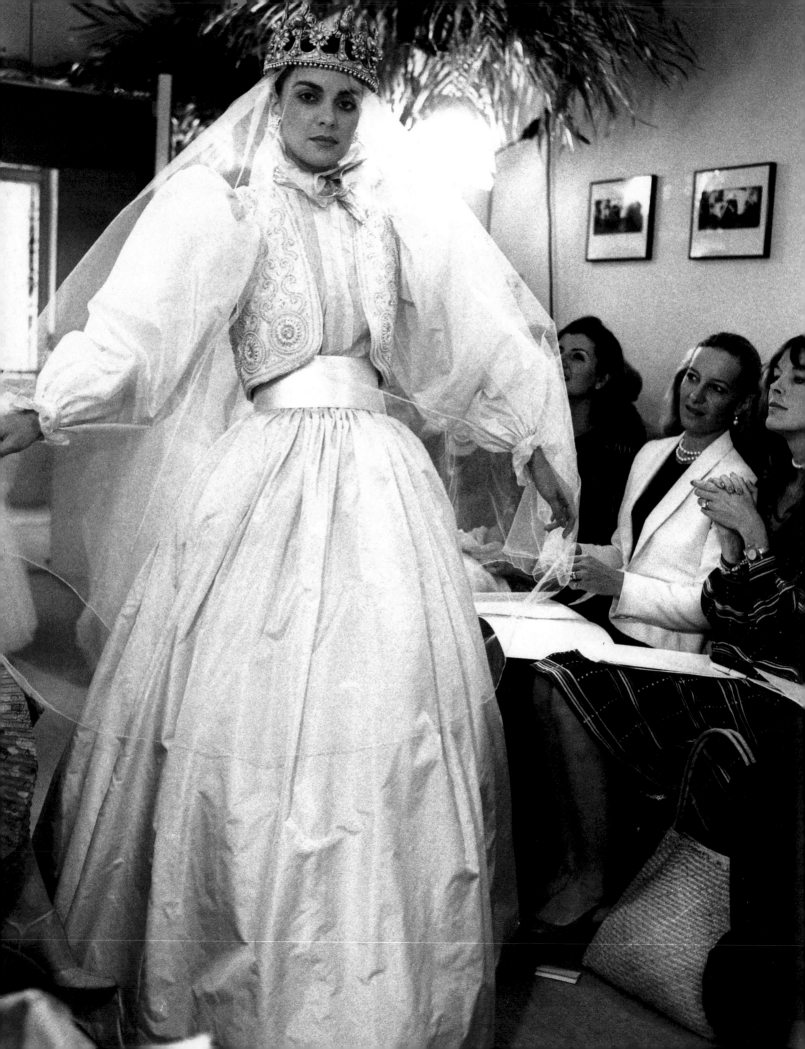

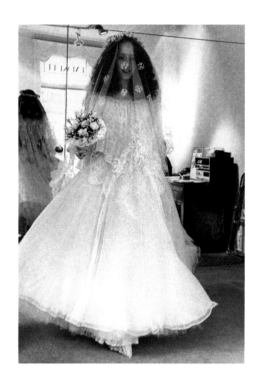

THEY WERE DIFFERENT

... AT THE FIRST ...

... NESS OF SPIRIT ... AND

... WEDDING DRESS ...

... INDIVIDUAL ...

Opposite One of our first collections in the new showroom at
Brook Street featured a regal wedding gown in silk taffeta with
rich embroidery — an indication of what was to come? Looking
on are HRH Princess Michael of Kent and Arianna Stassinopoulos.

Above Another wedding dress from one of our early collections
showing the trademark Emanuel look.

Some of the first collection we designed after leaving the Royal College of Art was bought by Mrs Joan Burstein, who was – indeed still is – the owner of Browns in South Molton Street. She has an undisputed reputation for discovering new talent, and Browns, which was just round the corner from us, was one of the trendiest shops in London.

Bianca Jagger, who was one of Brown's customers, saw one of our dresses – all lace and chiffon, very romantic – and bought it. In fact, she wore this dress to the famous Studio 54 for her birthday party. She entered the night club on a white stallion, with a dove on her hand, and everybody went crazy. There were lots of pictures in the press. That dress had a very different look to anything that had been going on in fashion at the time and Bianca loved it so much that she wanted to find out where we were based. Somehow she managed to track us down and arrived at our front door, announcing into the intercom, "It's Bianca!"

We have Bianca to thank for attracting many clients to us in the early days. Undoubtedly, Bianca knew, and still knows, a lot of influential people, including royalty, nobility and celebrities. And what she wears is noticed. She also knows a lot of fashion designers and would tell us what they were doing. For example, we were making a fitted jacket for her and she commented, "Oh, of course, Yves cuts his sleeves like this." She was talking about Yves St. Laurent. We didn't mind learning from masters like that!

Following Bianca, everyone was suddenly coming to our door. There was Princess Lowenstein, Carolina Herrera (now a fashion designer herself in New York), HRH Princess Michael of Kent, and then HRH The Duchess of Kent. (For many years we designed her entire wardrobe of daywear, cocktail and evening wear, and from her we learnt what the requirements were for a Royal.) Meanwhile, Lynne Wyatt, wife of a Texan billionaire, and other style gurus were also rushing to us because they all loved the thought of discovering something new. It was such an exciting time for us: we were barely out of college and suddenly we had become flavour of the month.

"The following day, it was in the press that Mrs Jagger was wearing a Dior gown. We were incredibly flattered: we'd been out of college for only a few months and they thought that our dress was a Dior. We were terribly touched."

Opposite Bianca Jagger at a party at Claridges to celebrate Princess Margaret's birthday, looking divine with movie star Jack Nicholson and wearing one of our dresses!

Overleaf We decided that it would be fun to keep visitors' books and found these amazing burgundy leather-bound albums at Smythsons in Bond Street, just round the corner from our studio.

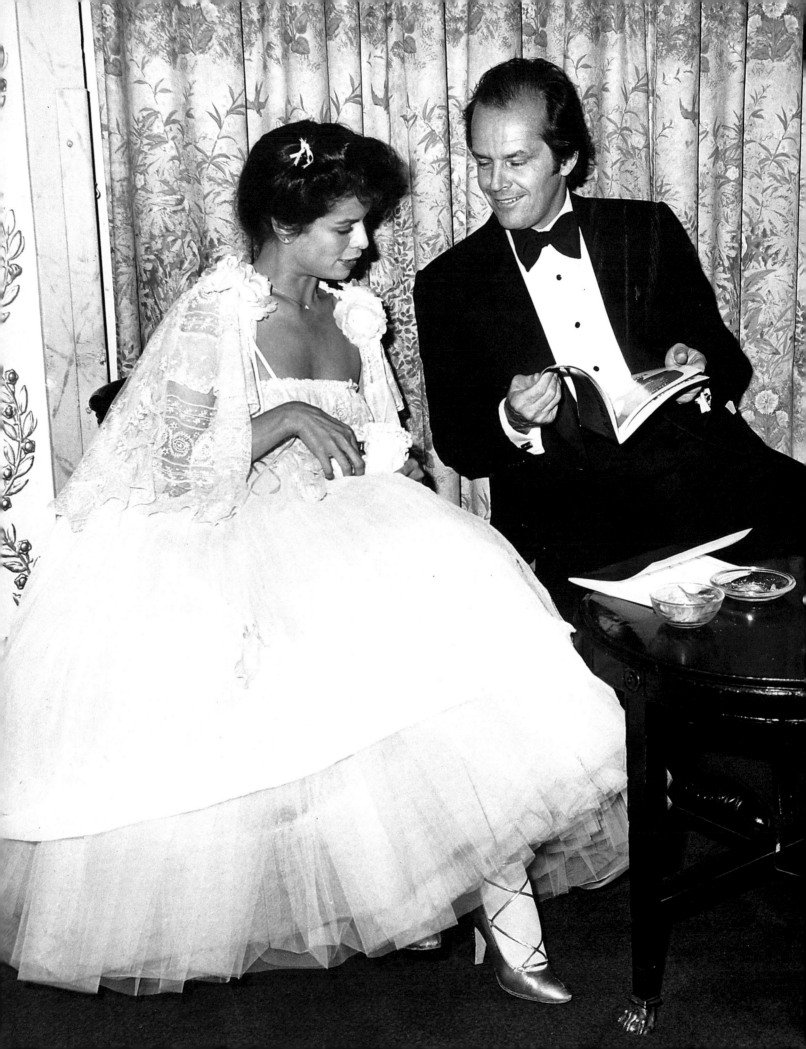

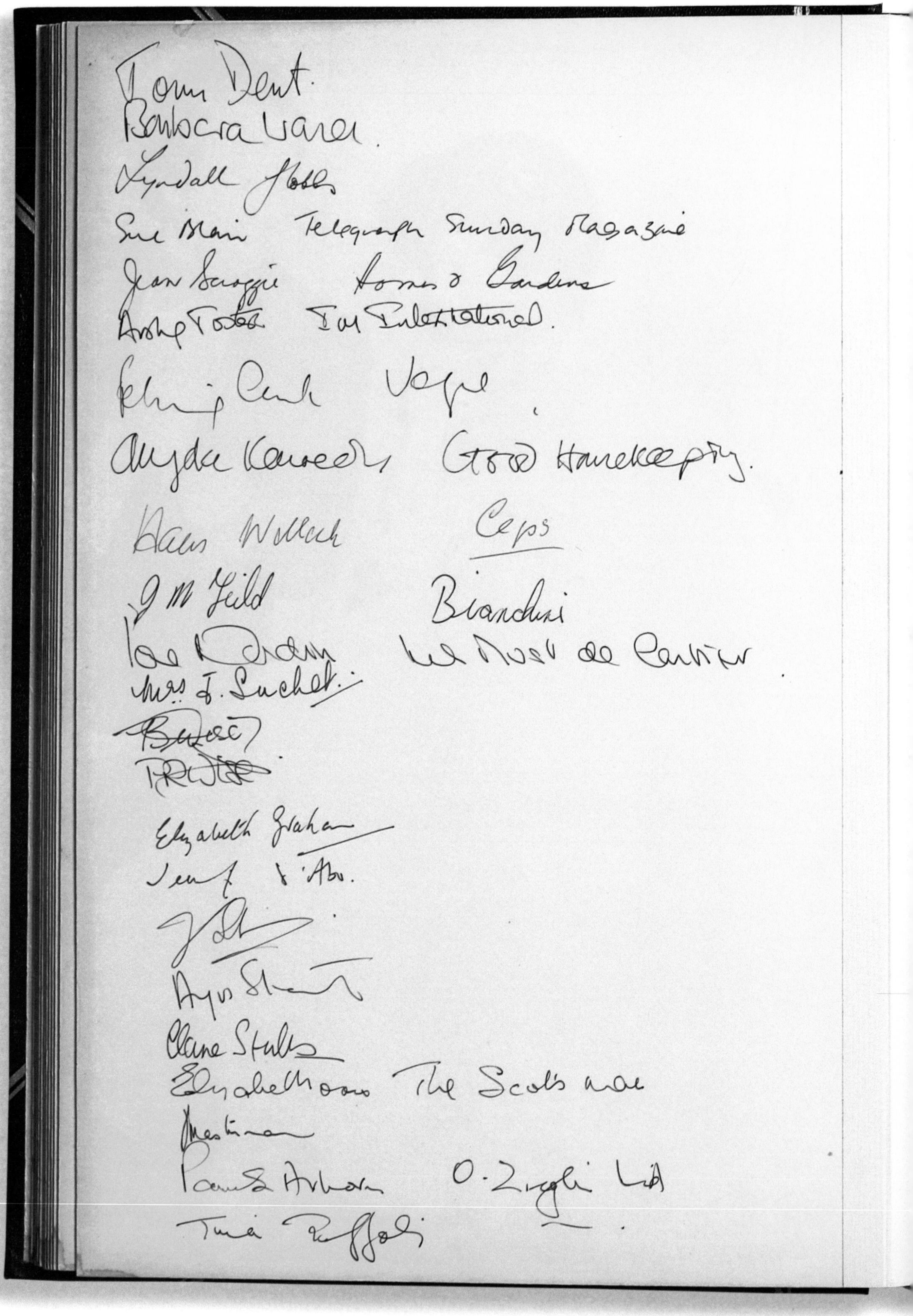

Tom Dent.

Barbara Varela

Lyndall Hobbs

Sue Main   Telegraph Sunday Magazine

Jean Scroggie   Homes & Gardens

Aretha Foster   TWA International.

Philip Clark   Vogue

Angela Kennedy   Good Housekeeping.

Daniel Wollach   Ceps

J M Field   Bianchini

Ian Cordery   Le Nose de Cartier

Mrs J. Suchet.

[signature]
[signature].

Elizabeth Graham

Jenny d'Abo.

[signature].

Angus Stewart

Claire Stubbs

Elizabeth Owen   The Scots mae

[signature]

Pamela Arbour   O. Ziegli Ltd

Tina Ruffoli

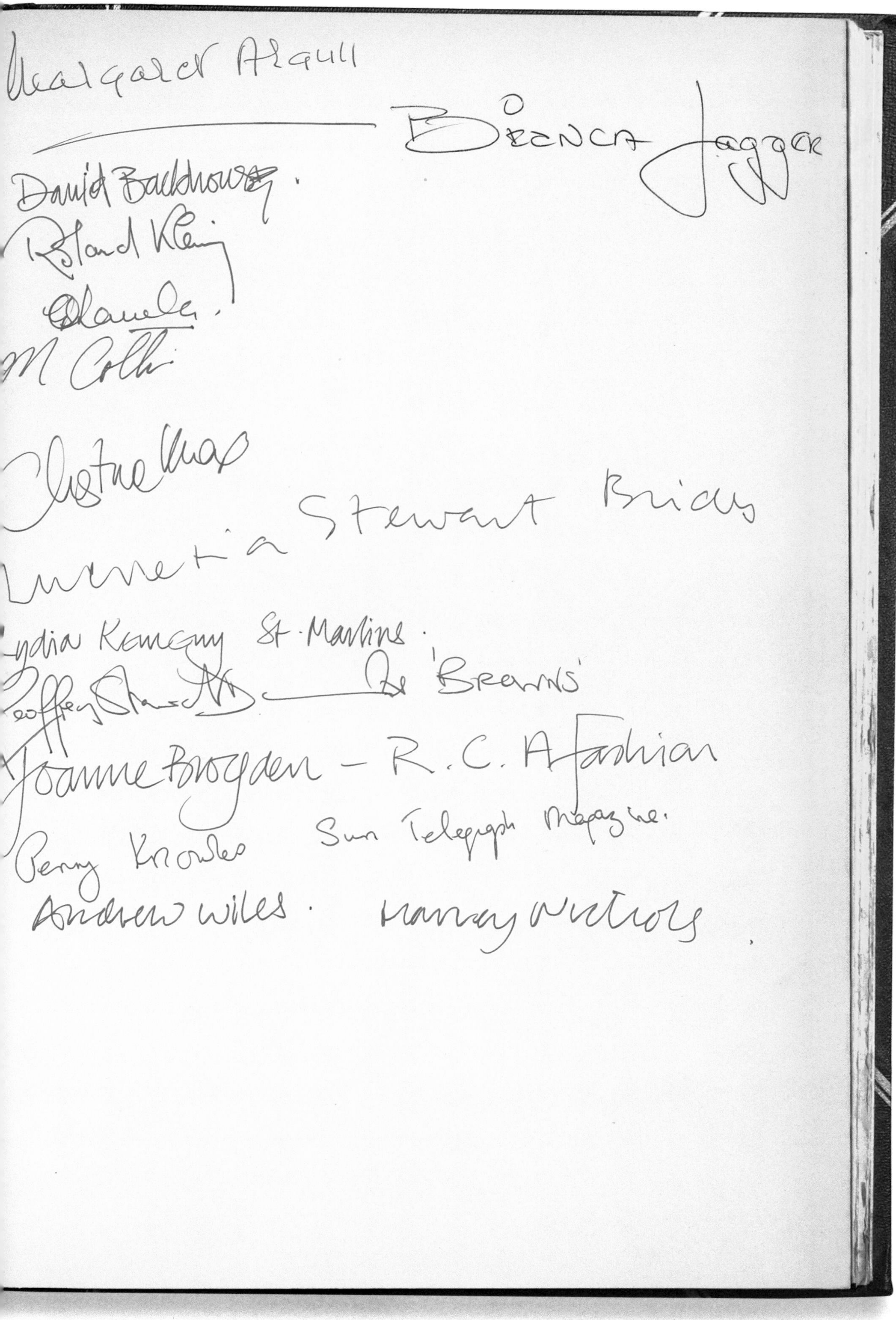

Margaret Argull

Bianca Jagger

David Backhouse.

Roland Klein

Chanelle.

M Colli

Christine May

Lucretia Stewart Bricks

Lydia Kemeny St. Martins.

Geoffrey Shaw Re 'Browns'

Joanne Brogden — R.C.A Fashion

Penny Knowles   Sun Telegraph Magazine.

Andrew Wiles.   Harvey Nichols

Emanuel's association with *Vogue* goes right back to the very beginning. One of *Vogue*'s Fashion Editors at the time was Anna Harvey and she had come to see our show at the Royal College of Art. She was impressed and followed us to Brook Street, where she attended our very first opening. (Little did she know that we were frantically laying the carpet only fifteen minutes before the show began!) We had two model girls, but because space was in short supply one of them would have to change in the back while the other one was showing up front.

Emanuel's introduction into *Vogue* was six pages of daywear featured in black-and-white editorial, which was a very good start for fledgling designers. Anna Harvey was a great mentor to us, helping us, guiding us and encouraging us in our first steps into the fashion world.

Because we were situated so close to Vogue House, the fashion team would often phone us to ask whether we could help them out with a particular garment. If we could supply them with a long, pink dress, for example, they would be spared the time they would otherwise have spent rushing round the shops trying to find something suitable. Sometimes we would make things up specially for them, which we would then drop round to their offices or which they would call in and collect. The arrangement suited both of us: we saved them time and hassle and in return they took wonderful pictures of our dresses, which were featured in *Vogue*.

There were other benefits too. Beatrix Miller, who was at that time the Editor of *Vogue*, came in to visit us one day and told us that she would like to bring HRH Princess Michael in to meet us. She also introduced us to many other members of the Royal family and by the time we received the Royal wedding dress commission we were dressing many of them as well as lots of celebrities. And, of course, because *Vogue* is *the* fashion magazine, when Lady Diana Spencer came into the public eye, it became virtually part of Anna Harvey's job to look after her.

Above right Lady Diana Spencer cautiously poses for press photographers and journalists shortly after her engagement to HRH The Prince of Wales is announced.
Above left In our office at Brook Street. We soon became used to having our picture taken!

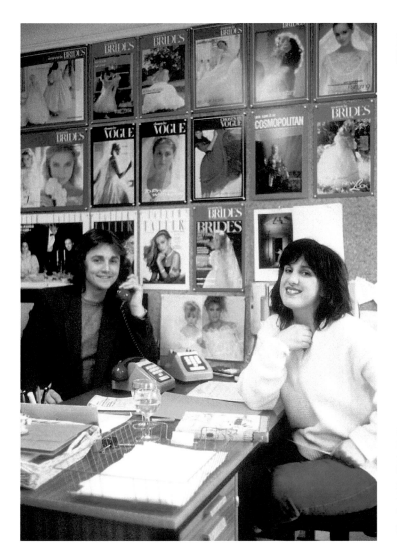 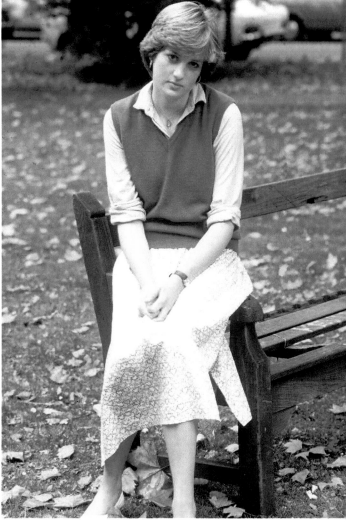

"David and I looked so young in those first pictures and we were scarcely out of college when we first met Diana. That first meeting changed out lives forever. We felt great affinity with her because were all young, naive and completely out of our depth!"

THE PINK BLOUSE

As always, fashion lovers everywhere were watching British *Vogue* to keep up with the latest fashions. One day, we received a phone call from *Vogue* telling us that they were doing a feature on upcoming beauties and wondering, as was quite common, whether we could help them out with any suitable clothes for the photo shoot. Naturally we asked them who the beauty was, but they declined to answer. When they wouldn't even tell us whether she was blonde or dark, we realized that this must be something important.

As it happened, we had recently seen a client who had wanted a pale pink skirt made. Unfortunately, when she had tried it on, she had somehow got mascara over it and rather than try and clean it we had decided to make her a new one. We had put the marked skirt to one side and later modified it and created a pink chiffon blouse to go with it.

It was this blouse that was hanging up in our studio when we suddenly received the phone call from *Vogue* requesting something which had a high neck and was very romantic. It was only later that we discovered that the blouse had been worn by Lady Diana (whose sisters had both worked at *Vogue*). The fashion team had assembled a large collection of clothes from several designers for her to try, just as you would for any fashion or beauty shoot. When she saw our blouse on the rack she fell in love with it, asked who had made it and was directed to us. That was the beginning of our relationship with Diana. Fortuitously, the engagement between Prince Charles and Lady Diana was announced shortly after that shoot and this picture (shown opposite), taken by Lord Snowdon, was used as the engagement photograph.

"In part, no doubt, thanks to that photograph, Emanuel began to be used as an adjective in the fashion world – 'Oh, it's very Emanuel', 'It has an Emanuel feel about it' – and looking back it seems we helped to usher in the enormous romantic movement in fashion of the early 1980s."

Opposite Lord Snowdon's official engagement photograph. This was the blouse that Diana fell in love with and influenced her decision to appoint us as her wedding dress designers.

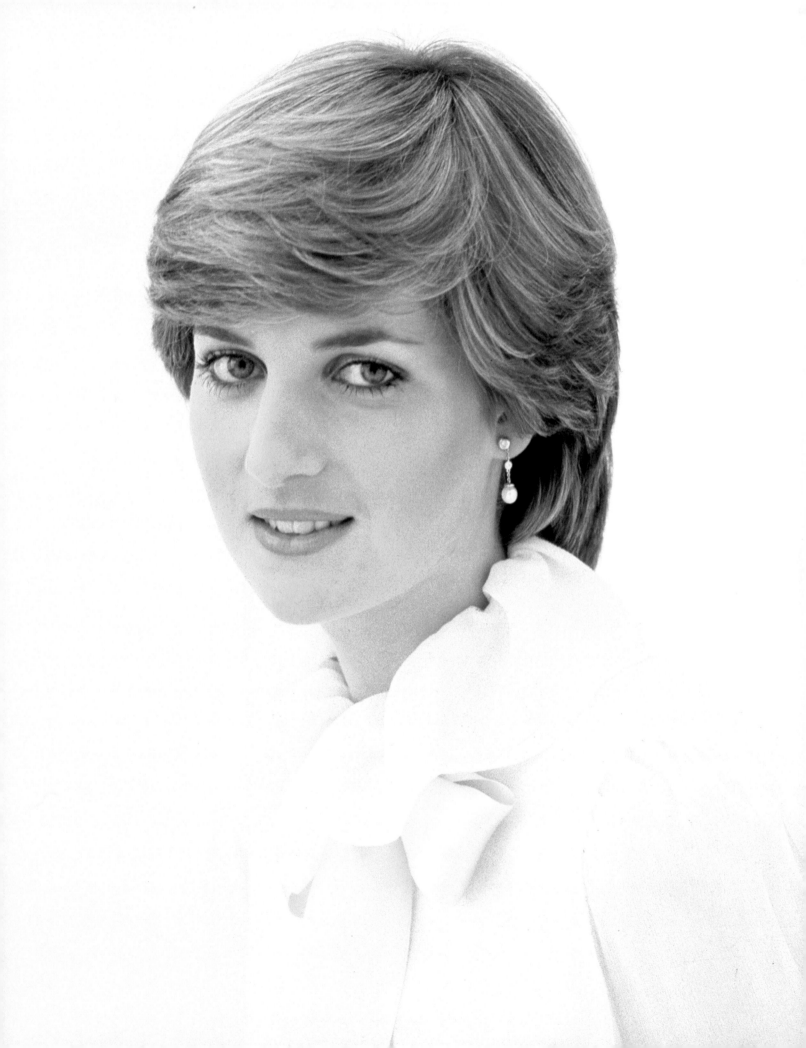

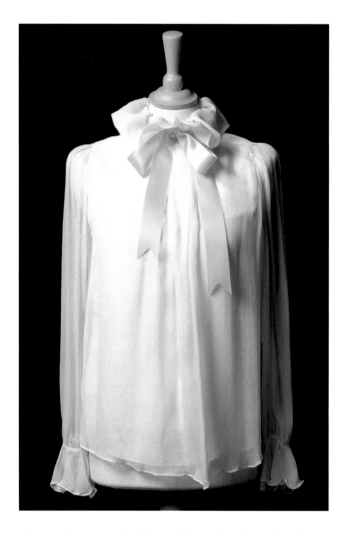

Above and opposite The Emanuel blouse that Diana chose for the
Vogue shoot was made from the palest pink silk chiffon supplied
by the silk merchant Henry Bertrand, which had a slight crinkle
in it. The style of the blouse was very gentle and romantic, it had
a soft floaty collar, and we had used a piece of very pale pink silk
satin ribbon as a bow.

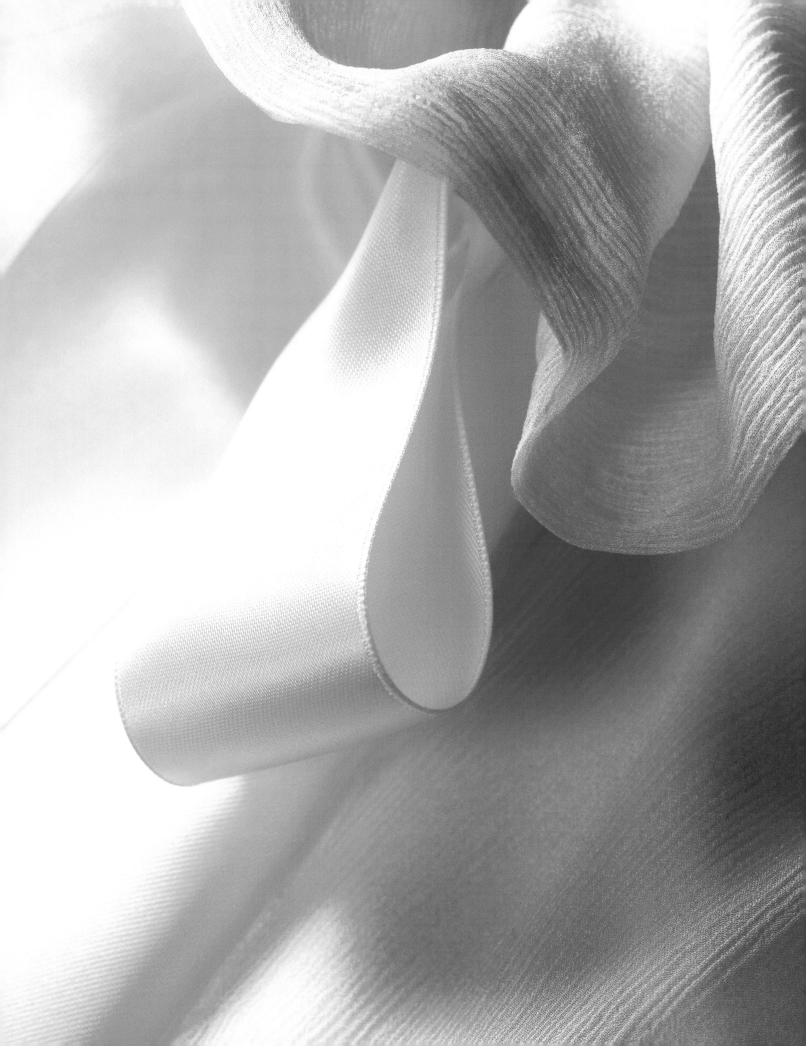

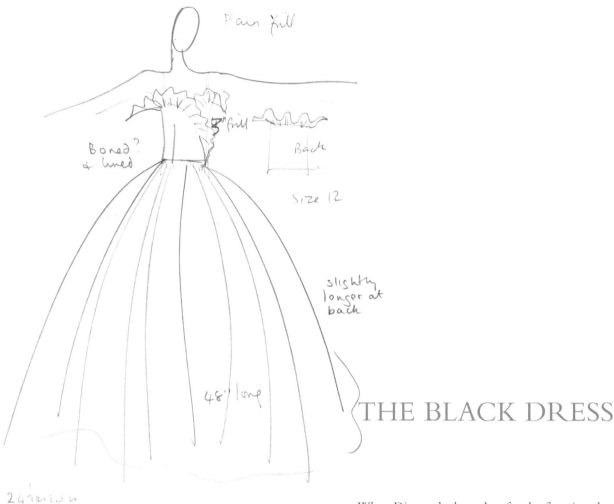

Plain frill

3" frill

Back

Size 12

Boned?
+ lined

slightly
longer at
back

48" long

THE BLACK DRESS

Above and opposite Sketches for the black dress that Diana wore on her first public engagement with HRH The Prince of Wales. The dress, made from black silk taffeta, was embroidered with black sequins and had a tight corseted bodice and a full gathered skirt that enhaced Diana's womanly curves. It caused a big stir!

When Diana telephoned us for the first time, her name was written down incorrectly, so when she came in for the appointment we were totally taken aback. By this time, she was making big news – there was a lot of speculation about her relationship with Prince Charles. We didn't know, until she casually let slip at our meeting, that she had been photographed for Vogue. What immediately struck us was her height, her beautiful blue eyes and her flawless complexion. She was a breath of fresh air – shy, unaffected and lovely.

On one of her increasingly frequent visits, after the formal announcement of her engagement to HRH The Prince of Wales, she needed a very grown-up dress for their first public engagement at Goldsmiths' Hall. We asked her, "Is it a black tie event" and she replied, "I think so". It was all entirely new for her.

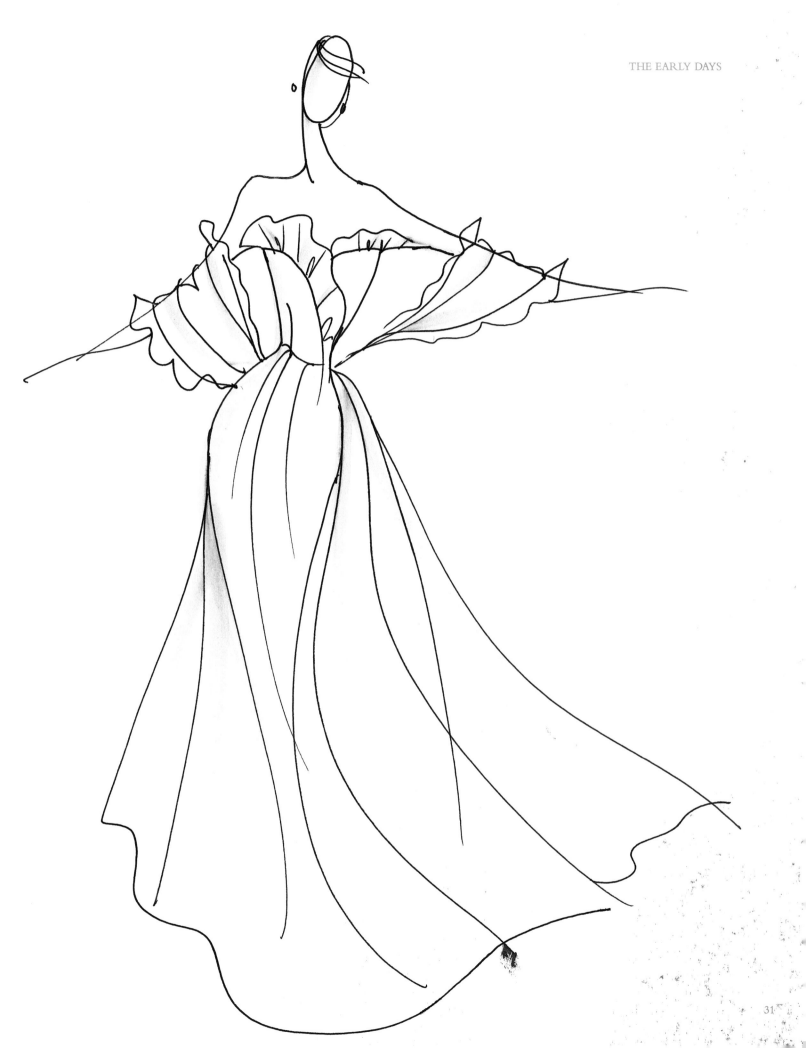

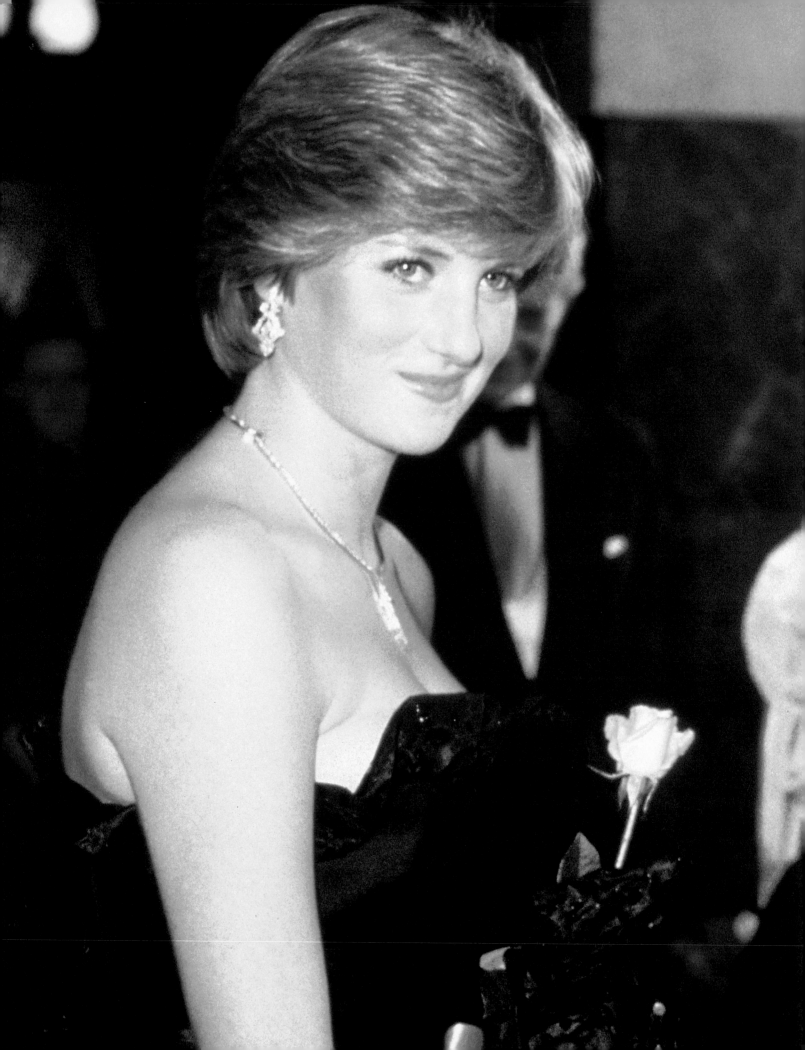

"That black dress changed the public's perception of Diana overnight. One minute she was a young nursery school teacher and the next she was a fully fledged princess in waiting. It was astounding - the birth of a fashion icon before our very eyes."

When we put her in that black dress, we had no idea that it was going to cause such a furore. In fact, that dress had started its life as one of our samples and it was just hanging on a rail. We had already lent it out to the actress Liza Goddard, so it wasn't even new. But Diana saw it, loved it and tried it on. The transformation was incredible! She had arrived looking like the nursery school teacher she was, but now she looked like a movie star. We gave her the dress, made a little shawl to go with it so she could cover up on the night, and away she went.

We hadn't considered the fact that when Diana bent over – as she would have to do when getting out of the car – she would show quite a lot of cleavage. We just thought she looked just fabulous.

The pictures of that evening show Diana stepping out of a limousine with HRH The Prince of Wales, looking like a movie star. This was a time when the country was aching for some romance, some glamour. And here was a beautiful woman in a beautiful dress escorting the heir to the throne. Prince Charles had finally met his princess.

The following day was Budget Day, but all news of the Budget was shifted into the middle of the newspaper to make room for pictures of Diana in that black dress.

"AS PRINCE CHARLES GOT OUT OF THE CAR FIRST, HE TURNED TO US
AND SAID 'YOU WANT TO SEE WHAT'S COMING NEXT', AND HE WAS
RIGHT. SHE LOOKED A MILLION DOLLARS."

Arthur Edwards, royal photographer

Opposite The infamous photo of Diana arriving at Goldsmiths
Hall and stepping out her limousine in our black dress. We
hadn't realized that, on leaning over, she would reveal quite
so much cleavage.

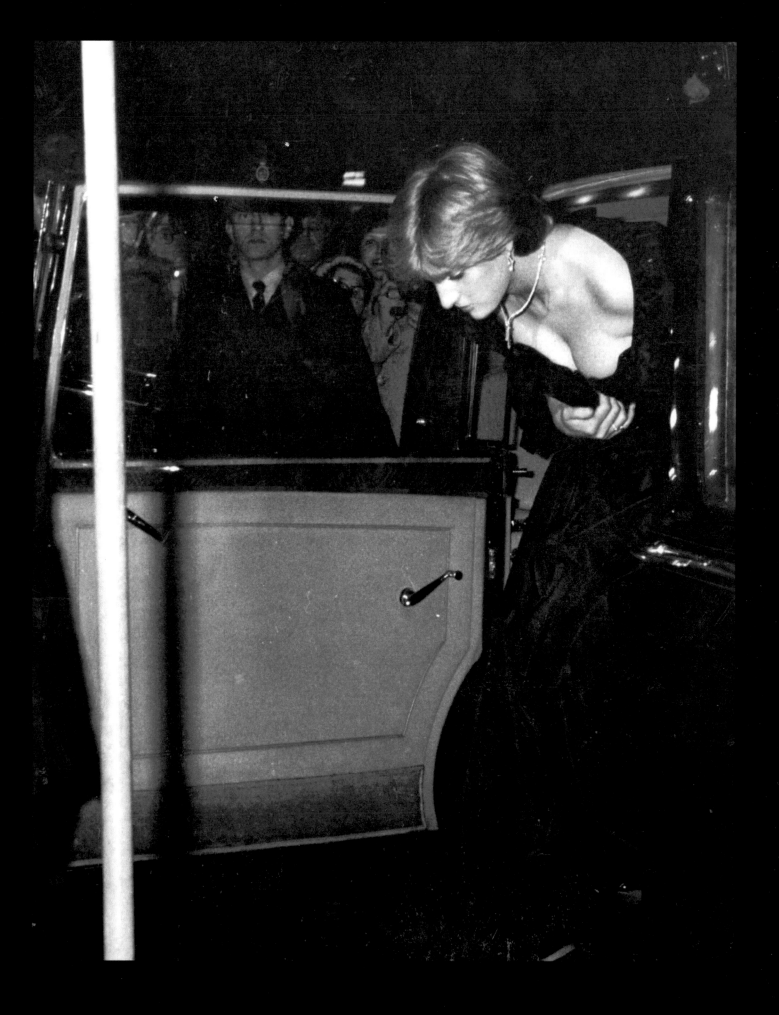

"WE RAN A SPECIAL EDITION ON ROYAL WEDDINGS AND ASKED SIX TOP DESIGNERS TO SUBMIT THEIR IDEAS FOR A ROYAL WEDDING DRESS. THE EMANUELS WERE ASKED, ALONG WITH ZANDRA RHODES, HARDY AMIES, BELLVILLE SASSOON, JEAN MUIR AND BILL GIBB. IF YOU LOOK AT THE EMANUELS DESIGN, IT WAS VERY CLOSE IN STYLE TO THE FINISHED DRESS. DIANA WAS IN A 'FRILLY PHASE', TYPICAL OF THE FASHIONS AT THE TIME, SO ELIZABETH'S DESIGNS VERY MUCH SUITED THAT TASTE."

Felicity Clarke, former Beauty Editor of *Vogue*

Opposite *Vogue* asked a number of fashion designers "If you could design a dress for Lady Diana, what would it look like?" This was our proposal, which was featured in the magazine. The dress we actually made was similar to this one in many aspects.

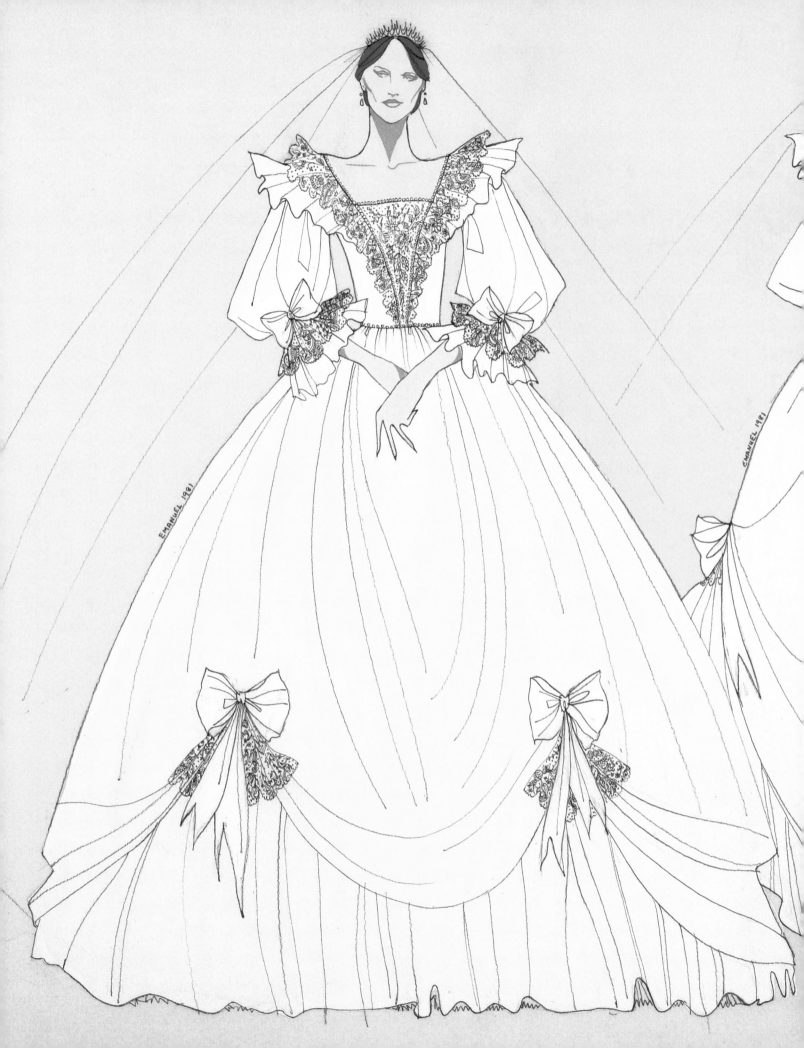

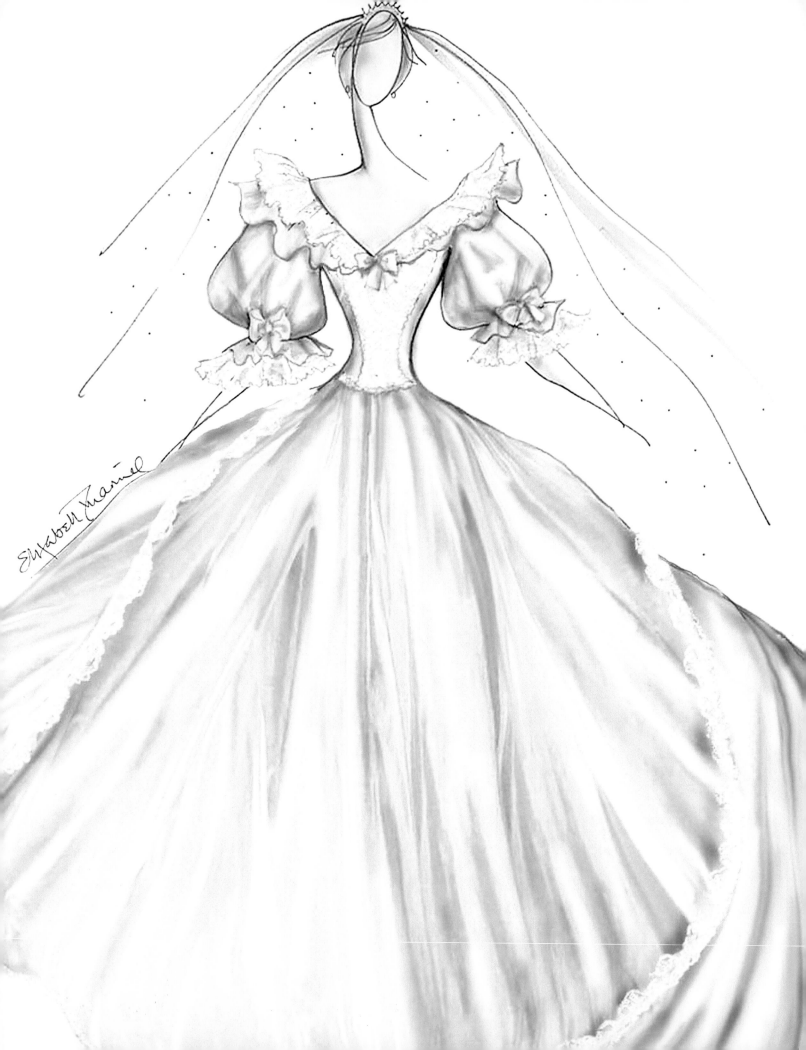

THE COMMISSION

Elizabeth was in the showroom dressing one of our clients – a real rock-and-roll girl, who was getting married to her record producer fiancé. The phone was ringing and ringing and no-one was answering it. Eventually, Elizabeth picked it up and a voice said simply, "This is Diana. I was wondering...", there was a pause, "Liz, would you and David do me the honour of making my wedding dress."

Making up some story about her brother's wife having just given birth, Elizabeth excused herself and rushed excitedly from the room, leaving the poor girl wearing nothing but a whisp of chiffon. The bewildered client must have heard us clapping our hands, whooping for joy and jumping up and down as Elizabeth shared the news, but fortunately we managed to keep the true reasons for our celebrations a secret.

Although it was wonderful sharing the news with everyone in the studio, the person Elizabeth was most keen to tell was her father, who was unfortunately very ill in hospital at the time. We were worried that the excitement might be dangerous for his heart condition, but he had given us so much support and encouragement with the business that we decided he would want to know. He was naturally delighted for us and even had the foresight to say "Don't forget to charge VAT" – a true businessman!

There was so much press speculation at the time about who was going to design the dress that when we didn't hear anything more, we were almost tempted to believe we had been the victims of a hoax. Could it really be true? It wasn't until Diana rang us a few days later that we were able to ask her, "Do you really want us to do this?" "Of course," she replied. "Well you'd better come in then", we said. So she came in to see us at Brook Street and we began our discussions about the dress. It was a most extraordinary time.

"I picked up the phone and it was Diana and I froze. She just said 'Would you and David do me the honour of making my wedding dress?' It was the most exciting moment of my life."

Opposite Our waiting room at Brook Street.

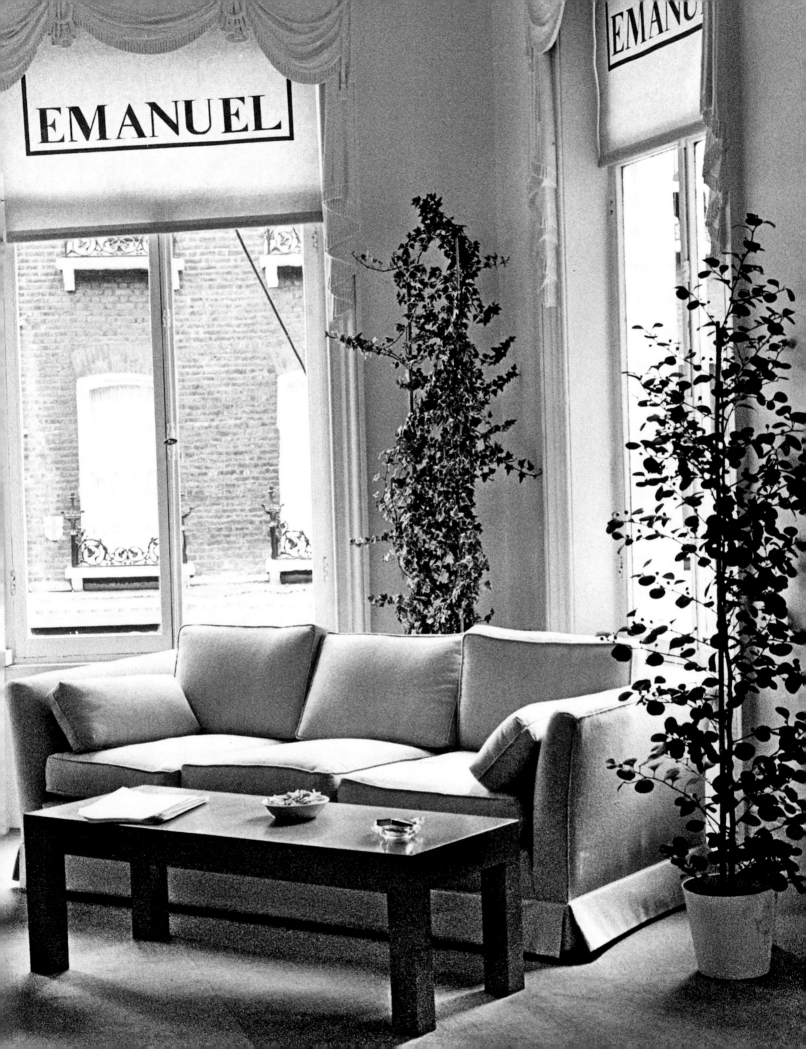

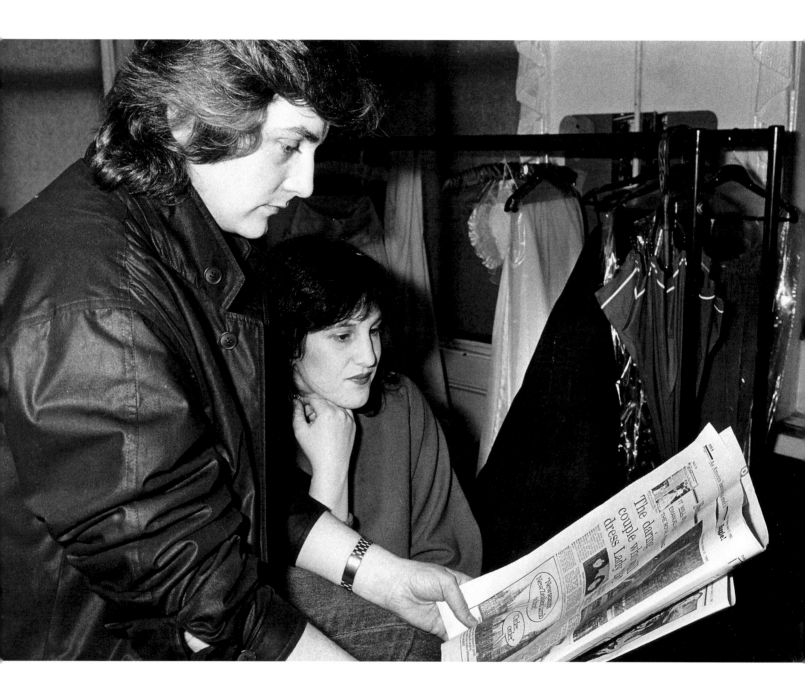

During the waiting period, after receiving the initial call from Diana but before the official announcement was made that we had been chosen to design the dress, we had to live with all sorts of rumours about who had been selected, and that was difficult for us. After all, although we had quickly gathered quite a following, we were still very much newcomers: we were known by the *Vogue* set, some of the royal set, the social set, but we definitely weren't known across the country. And we were very fresh out of college. Of course, the press were making all sorts of speculations about who had been chosen to design the dress: some said Zandra Rhodes, others favoured Sir Hardy Amies (for whom David had worked as a student and who was dressmaker by appointment to HM The Queen).

And of course, we had to keep the commission a seccret; we couldn't tell anybody else. (Once the news broke, we had to carefully guard against anyone finding out anything about the design, of dress, so this was good practice for us!) The girls in the workroom knew what was happening, but they had been been sworn to secrecy. We trusted them completely, and they never let us down.

Finally, on 10 March, we received a phone call from the Press Office at Buckingham Palace. This time, it was David who answered the call. He was told, "Mr Emanuel, at midday today it will be formally announced that you and Elizabeth will be making Lady Diana's wedding gown." At that point, we decided that it was safe to crack open a bottle of Champagne.

Opposite Reading all about our commission in the London *Evening Standard* on the afternoon of 10 March 1981.

THE PRESS

And then it all happened. All hell broke loose. Once the formal announcement had been made, we were beseiged by what seemed like every film crew in the world. In our tiny little four-storey studio, we didn't have anything like enough room to do a grand press announcement. So instead, each film crew had to come in separately and set up their lights and do their various interviews. We spent an exhausting day telling different journalists how flattered and honoured and excited we were.

But at the end of the day, they didn't go away. And on the following day we noted that there were photographers with paparazzi-type lenses on the roofs of the buildings opposite. In fact, the press stayed and they stayed and they stayed. We literally had journalists camped out from day one – they were outside our front door and on the roofs, taking any pictures they could of people coming and going. Of course, they were particularly hungry to find out when Diana was coming for an appointment. One of our first assignments was to run out and buy roller blinds for every one of the windows, to protect ourselves – and more importantly the dress – from the prying eyes of the press.

Being invaded by the press was obviously difficult, particularly at first, and secrecy was paramount. We later discovered that our team had been offered huge sums of cash by tabloid journalists in exchange for any information at all about the dress. But no details were ever leaked.

Although no-one could have predicted what a major news story the wedding and the dress would turn out to be, it was somewhat perplexing that we were never given any kind of advice by Buckingham Palace. We were designing the most important dress of the century and we were just left to our own devices. However, we obviously weren't going far wrong, because a week later Buckingham Palace Press Secretary, Michael Shea, rang to say "Congratulations – keep up the good work".

"That day changed our lives. In an instant we were transformed from naive young graduates just embarking on our career to designers whose work was about to be seen and judged by a television audience of more than 800 million people. Scary stuff!"

Opposite Just some of the newspaper and magazine articles speculating on what Diana would be wearing on the big day – but we were determined to keep it a secret.

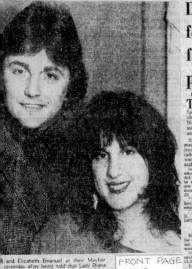

Dress for a fairy princess

By WINIFRED CARR

THE wedding dress that Lady Diana Spencer will wear when she marries the Prince of Wales in July will be made by David Emanuel and his wife, Elizabeth.

It was the Emanuels who made the spectacular strapless gown in black silk taffeta which Lady Diana wore to a gala on Monday night.

David, 28, and Elizabeth, 27, who left the Royal College of Art less than three years ago to set up a salon in Mayfair, are planning a "romantic" dress for the wedding on July 29.

"She is young, fresh and lovely and the dress should emphasise all that," said David. "We are very excited about it. We want to make her look a fairy princess."

£1,500 upwards

He said the procedure was for the bride to visit the salon for discussions and then she would be sent a quotation.

No price was mentioned, but outfits cost anything from £1,500.

Lady Diana was introduced to the couturiers by Vogue last year when Lord Snowdon photographed her for the magazine.

She visited the salon last week to find a dress for last Monday's gala, her first public engagement with Prince Charles and selected the black dress that has put fashion circles in a spin.

The daring couple who will dress Lady Di!

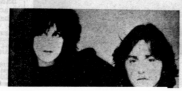

LADY Diana Spencer's wedding dress will be designed by the husband - and - wife team of David and Elizabeth Emanuel, who also designed the stunning, strapless black ballgown she wore so...

by JEAN DOBSON and ANDREW McEWAN

top of the fashion world and proves that there is a wind of change blowing through the industry — and it's a tremendous departure from the stately classic Royal wedding dresses designed by old masters such as Norman Hartnell.

Sitting in their workrooms while telephones were constantly ringing yesterday with congratulations, Liz Emanuel refused to be drawn on any details of Lady Diana's wedding dress.

Secret

'There won't be a sketch for this dress,' she said, 'It will be the best-kept secret ever.'

Over the last few years the Emanuels have gradually been gaining acclaim as the best designers of daring fairytale ballgowns and wedding dresses.

From previous Emanuel wedding dresses it seems likely that Lady Diana's dress will be along these lines:

NECKLINE: off-the-shoulder ruffles rather than the traditional demure neckline.

BODICE: Figure-hugging, possibly with swirls of net decoration.

WAIST: Small, sashed with a big bow at the...

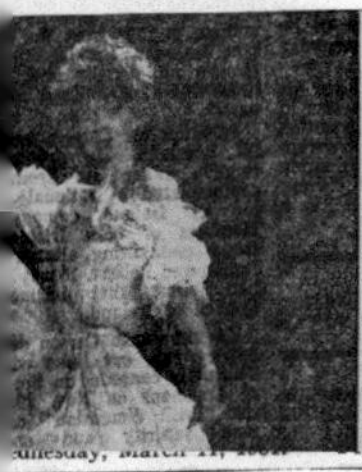

SETTING NEW ROYAL STYLE

BY ANN CHUBB

THE choice of London's youngest couturiers, Elizabeth and David Emanuel, to design Lady Diana Spencer's wedding dress is certainly a popular one.

At 27 and 28, this personable, young and rather shy couple are well loved by the fashion world who admire not only their talent, but their discretion, which far belies their years. Coincidentally, one half of the partnership is Welsh—David is one of 11 sons of a Bridgend ex-steelworker—so who more apt to dress the new Princess of Wales?

The Emanuels met and married as...

Lady Diana's appearance in her spectacular strapless Emanuel ballgown of black silk taffeta decorated with diamanté, at the Royal Opera House's Gala of the Goldsmiths' Hall, the announcement epitomises Lady Diana's determination to break with tradition and to set Royal fashion—and young fashion at that.

As a 19-year-old newcomer to the Royal family, it would have been all too easy to bow to tradition. She stood fast and showed on Monday night just how glamorous and sophisticated she can look. It's rare for the...

wedding dress is likely to feature a crinoline and l...

return to rom...

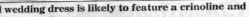

...Smith, Editor

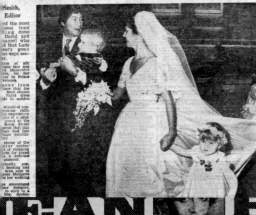

of the most ...ious from ...ding dress ...David and ...anuel who ...d that Lady ...r's gown ...t-kept sec...

...tion of silk ...e face was ...f Mancroft's ...for her for the Prince ...resses.

...ews from ...ace that she ...been chosen ...Royal dress ...le to sudden

...stress of com...mise calls ...e emancern...ce of a crin... at the Royal ...Brook Street ...dthat this ...on had just ...ange entirely ...n of the ...lter confec...of whipping ...rns for grand ...a welcome ...lamour.

...rtnell's pen...beeding and ...been kept in ...een Margaret ...her wedding ...been off.

...e encourag... designers, ...been off.

...it off to Prince ...le double-

Designing the 'dress of the decade' for Lady Diana

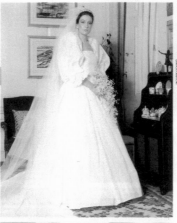

Kathryn Samuel charts the rapid rise to fame of couturiers David and Elizabeth Emanuel (above)

"She will look like a fairy tale princess." That is how David and Elizabeth Emanuel describe their early aims on the dress Lady Diana Spencer will wear for her wedding in July. Further discussion is taboo. "It is," David told me as I sat talking to the couple in their simple yet elegant Brook Street showroom, "the biggest secret we will ever have to keep."

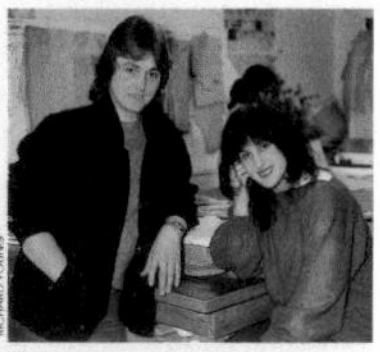

Indeed, it was the first interview they had given since the announcement that they were to design the dress for the future Princess of Wales. "As yet," said David, "we don't know whether we will be asked to design her 'going away' outfit. Obviously we would love to, but we are very thrilled and honoured merely to be doing her dress."

Lady Diana is a comparatively new Emanuel customer. It was just before Christmas, after she was photographed by Lord Snowdon for Vogue wearing an Emanuel blouse, that she was introduced to the couple. She popped into their showroom and ordered a dress she has yet to be seen wearing in public — the black taffeta strapless stunner she wore on her first official engagement was a later addition.

But Lady Diana can have been no stranger to the Emanuel style. Since David and Elizabeth left the Royal College of Art in 1977, the stars of their year, and set up their own business later that summer, they have been responsible for the dresses of many of the more fashion conscious society brides.

Emanuel style is distinctive. The very fact Lady Diana has chosen them rather than any other designer gives many strong clues as to

how the dress — and Lady Diana herself — will look on the wedding day.

The finale of their last show in mid-February featured a sensational wedding dress that summed up much of the essence of their flair.

It was called, appropriately enough, Fairy Princess. A splendid theatrical confection in white silk taffeta with a majestic full skirt buoyed up with acres of net petticoat, the sleeves were puffed and long and the neckline deep and frilled.

Past Emanuel ball and wedding dresses have that same dramatic presence; they are boldly feminine and in fabrics that can only be described as the most sumptuous.

This talented couple will not disappoint Lady Diana or the rest of the watching world. Her dress will be, as it is already being dubbed, the Dress of the Decade — adjectives like classic, simple or demure will not be at all relevant, I suspect.

Lady Diana's choice of designer appears to be a universally popular one. The fact that the Emanuels are both young — Elizabeth is 27 and David just a year older — and in international terms comparatively unknown will, it is felt, give a great fillip to the British fashion industry.

David was born in Bridgend, Glamorgan, one of a family of nine sons and one sister. His father, now retired, was a steel worker, his mother still runs a bookshop in the town.

In the Welsh tradition, he was musical and, before going to college in Cardiff to do fashion, played the violin in the Glamorgan Youth Orchestra and sang in the choir. "I meant I could be in both halves of the programme," he says.

David met Elizabeth when he moved to Harrow College of Art to complete his final year. She admits to setting her cap at him

continued on page 20

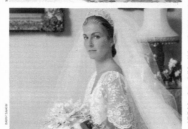

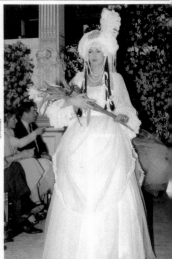

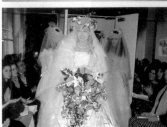

ABOVE LEFT: The Emanuels designed a dress of sequinned tulle for Candid Howard last February
LEFT: Taffeta and lace for Victoria Mancroft in February 1980

ABOVE RIGHT: An Emanuel creation for a fashion show at the British Embassy in Paris last March
RIGHT: For Liberty's Silk Cut collection, now in the Victoria and Albert museum

NOW MARCH 20, 1981

Daring Diana—she's all things bold and beautiful

LADY DI literally plunged into public life. Bounced into the spotlight. Gave Britain the uplift it needs. And caused cleavage among members of the public, who took one gasp at her sensational, strapless black taffeta dress and dived for the phone to Buck House.

Within seconds of Daring Di's first official public exposure on TV news, the Palace switchboard was jiggling with calls from people who loved every inch of Di, and would have liked even less of the dress.

And those who complained, holding their breath, that if she'd made one slip lower, bending to get out of the car, everything — including the engagement — could have been off.

I take it off to Prince Charles's fiancee for putting on a bold, beautiful front. And for turning her cold, bare shoulders on the traditional, covered-up royal evening dress.

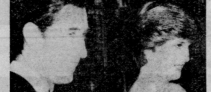

Charles and Di: Tradition gets cold shouldered

the bones stick like fish knives into your midriff.

All 19-year-old Di must learn to watch, which the TV cameras noticed, is the ounce or two of puppy fat which boned bodices tuck

been the first (you don't risk a dress like that without your future husband's assent) to have his breath snatched when she breathed out.

Designers David, 28, and Elizabeth, 27, who met 'at college and have two young children, refused to lay bare the price of the "one-off" dress which nobody else's money could buy— "it was just for her, and we'll never make another."

I reckon you wouldn't get many copies of the Queen's head out of £1,000.

The Emanuels don't sell wholesale, except at Lady Di's favourite shop, Harrods. But it was to their salon in Brook Street, Mayfair, that she went for what she called "something special, with a touch of fantasy" when Prince...

ling display of more than a diamond necklace.

"It certainly wasn't rude," they told me the morning after the lady's great first night. "It was very tasteful just right for...

DREAM FIT FOR A PRINCESS

Is this how Lady Di will look on her Royal wedding day?

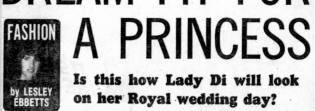

LADY Diana Spencer's wedding day will be a dream ome true for two young ashion designers.

For David Emanuel and his

wife Elizabeth are making her bridal dress—the "dress of the decade".

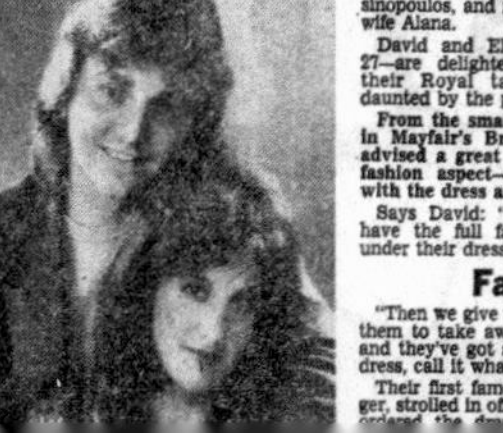

And when the Princess-to-be steps out on July 29, their joint creation will be seen by an estimated 500 million people round the world.

It's the pinnacle in a short but meteoric career of dressing the famous—among their clients are singer Lulu, writer and TV personality Arianna Stassinopoulos, and rock star Rod Stewart's wife Alana.

David and Elizabeth—he's 28, she's 27—are delighted and excited about their Royal task. But they're not daunted by the prospect.

From the small, exclusive showroom in Mayfair's Brook Street they have advised a great many brides on every fashion aspect—even on what to do with the dress afterwards.

Says David: "We tell our brides to have the full fairy-tale fantasy skirts under their dress for the big day.

"Then we give them a silk slip and tell them to take away the tulle petticoats and they've got a supper dress, evening dress, call it what they will, for later."

Their first famous client, Bianca Jagger, strolled in off the streets in 1978 and...

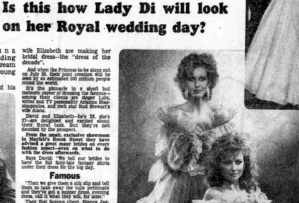

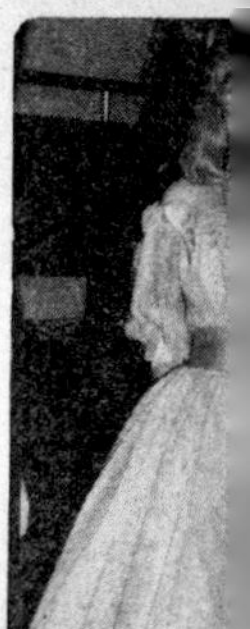

Thursday April 23rd
'We feel safe now' — our security guards have arrived
Elizabeth started embroidering lace
with sequins & pearls last night.
DEBRA CALICO toiles already fitted — but Nina working
on final toile in real fabric.

Girls completing D. of Kent outfit for
her to wear to Childrens H. Park
Charity Rally & Cup Final Day.

Rose busy finishing Elizabeth's blouse
(to wear to B.P. later this morning.
→ ALSO B. Bach. 2nd visit.
Went to B.P. & saw Debra & Mr
Everett. Walk through long red
corridor. Met & discussed bouquet &
B. maids flowers. All the people were a
bit stuffy!! But the Goodyear people
were on our wavelength. They
mentioned Madame Tussauds! HORROR!!

Came back to BARBARA Bach fitting.
+ PANIC. Our flower people delivered
on the shade of flowers. Christine Lefevre came
for clothes for
SHEENA EASTON.

Monday April 27
Delivered B. Bach outfit
Checked S. Hampshire outfit's
since she's opening soon in
W. End.
Elizabeth made divine supper
with John & him
Stefano & Atalanta Massimo.

Tuesday April 28th
Papers are full of B. Bach & Ringo's
wedding.

Paul, George & Ringo met!!
Our first batch of fabric arrived
NOW it's serious!!!

We rang St Pauls to find out
how wide is their aisle
spoke interview to June Weir
U.S.A. Vogue.
DEBRA rang to give more
B. maids info.

Friday April 24
Elizabeth & I
Rose & David Noel
Taxied to 'Securecode' for our
'mug-shots' security badges to
get into our own building.
Caroline & Charles went back—
Caroline _still_ won't show us her
Badge.
Rushed back for B. Bach's final
finals.
After lunch we went with
Irene to look at Sun-glass
people.
Delivered D. of Kent outfit to
S. J. Palace.

THE ALBUM

It wasn't really until we began to be interviewed by journalists that it fully dawned on us that what we were working on was going to be very, very significant. And at that point we made the decision that we should document the whole thing. We kept a diary and David bought a little camera and snapped away, taking photographs of the various processes throughout.

Initially we just wanted to create a memento for us, but later we realized that this would make a fabulous wedding present. Luckily, David had an uncle who worked at Kodak and he discreetly arranged to process all the films for us. We put the pictures into two leather-bound albums, wrote some cryptic little by-lines under each one and presented one to Charles and Diana as a wedding gift.

BY APPOINTMENT
TO HER MAJESTY
QUEEN ELIZABETH II
DRESSMAKERS

BY APPOINTMENT
TO H M QUEEN ELIZABETH
THE QUEEN MOTHER
DRESSMAKERS

· NORMAN **HARTNELL** LIMITED ·

REG. OFFICE

TELEPHONE
01-629 0992
(6 LINES)

REG No. 243083 ENGLAND

26 BRUTON STREET

LONDON · W · 1

12th March 1981

EMANUEL,
26a Brook Street,
W.1.

Dear Mr & Mrs Emanuel,
May I offer you my

congratulations on your good fortune in

receiving the order for the Wedding Dress

to be worn by Lady Diana Spencer.

I wish you every possible

success.

Yours sincerely,

George Mitchison

George Mitchison
Managing Director

LETTERS OF CONGRATULATION

Clearly, being asked to design this most important royal wedding dress was an honour that must have been coveted by every fashion designer in the country. Nevertheless, after the announcement was made, many designers who were much better known and established than we were at the time graciously wrote to us to offer their congratulations. Hardy Amies was dressmaker by appointment to Her Majesty the Queen, so might legitimately have expected to be asked. But the general consensus of opinion seemed to favour Bellville Sassoon. We felt humbled and overawed to receive such kind sentiments from these design greats.

BELLVILLE SASSOON

Dear David & Elizabeth, just to say Congratulations on the Dress I am thrilled for you both lots of Success with it all.
Much love David

Bellville Sassoon Limited 73 Pavilion Road London SW1 Telephone 01-235 3087 (Accounts 01-235 5801)

Opposite and above These letters of congratulation that we received from Norman Hartnell and Bellville Sassoon were only two of many that were sent to us by fashion designers and others after the announcement was made that we had been chosen to design the royal wedding dress.

EMANUEL

DAVID EMANUEL   ELIZABETH EMANUEL

When is the announcement to be made about the dress?

Will all the fabrics, trimmings, etc have to be British?

Is a special embroidered motif called for?

What sort of tiara will you be wearing?
We will need to view it at some stage to see the style and colours.

Who will be doing your hair?

Who will be supplying your shoes?

Where will the fittings be conducted?

What will HRH Prince Charles be wearing?

How many bridesmaids will there be and who are they?
How many pageboys will there be and who are they?
We will need their telephone numbers to arrange fittings.

Will Buckingham Palace arrange security or should we?

Whom should we contact at the Palace regarding any queries?

Can Siegel Stockman supply the stand?

26a BROOK STREET MAYFAIR LONDON W1   TELEPHONE 629 5560/5569

Above The commission to design the royal wedding gown had implications far beyond simply making a dress, and we were very new to all of this. We prepared these questions to ask Diana at the meeting we had with her and her mother, Mrs Shand Kydd.

Right We went to a meeting at Buckingham Palace with Diana and Oliver Everett, who became her Private Secretary, prepared with these questions. Some answers are scribbled beside them.

EMANUEL

DAVID EMANUEL   ELIZABETH EMANUEL

The Worshipful Company of Gardners for five

1. Security - any recommended firms?, payment, to start as soon as fabric arrives?

2. Itinerary for David & Liz for day of wedding (if dressing Lady Diana)

3. Lady Diana's dress & bridesmaids' dresses to be delivered to Clarence House when?

4. Will there be a canopy at St Paul's ? *from 8 us for rehearsal*

5. Will David & Liz attend the dress rehearsal at St Paul's on the Monday before the wedding? *YES.*

6. Do they know yet who will be doing the flowers? as we'd like to liaise with them.

7. We will need to see the tiara at some stage (or even a photo of it), and it will take a day to fix it to the veil. *majm before.*

8. List of credits and contributors (shoes, fabric, trimmings, etc) when can this information be released? The silk farm in particular are anxious to be able to make an announcement soon.

9. Will we have to release a sketch of the dress on the morning of the wedding? we would rather not if possible till afetrwards. *? ?*

10. Details regarding dress - Lindy wants to know WHEN this will be released (day or two before, or the day itself?) and to WHOM (will we discuss with B P Press Office which papers?). Will B P Press Office do this?

11. Sketches for HRH Princess Margaret - we would like to know decision soon if possible as to which sketch.

12- TV Documentary - before or after.

eased from police

THE DESIGN

We believe Diana chose us because the feel of Emanuel at the time was soft, pretty, romantic and very importantly youthful. But we knew that the dress we would create for her would also need to be grand enough to be a part of history. The prospect of designing the gown, though exciting, was also quite daunting. We didn't have any experience in designing *royal* wedding dresses. The extraordinary thing was that we weren't given any restrictions by the palace. There was no protocol. There wasn't even anything to say the dress had to be white.

In the end, the design process was quite simple because there were just the three of us: David, Elizabeth and Diana. We began by showing Diana all the dresses that we had samples of and we encouraged her to try them all on so that she could get an idea of what she felt comfortable in. She had never really worn anything quite like this kind of dress, so it was important for her to try on every single shape we had. She was terribly excited to be trying on huge bouffant petticoats, satin skirts and boned bodices, and she loved every minute of it.

Eventually, she settled on a style that looked fantastic. It had a frill at the shoulder, a tiny waist, a big skirt – very romantic – and we decided together that this shape would form the basis of the look we would create for her. The next thing we did was to draw up something like fifty different designs, but all based around the same silhouette.

"We were both very aware as designers that Diana was young and inexperienced, and that she was going to go into St Paul's as Lady Diana Spencer, but she would come out as the Princess of Wales, the wife of the heir to the throne."

Opposite This sample of one of the wedding dresses from an early Emanuel collection was photographed for several magazines. Diana tried it on when she first came in to see us to discuss her wedding dress and because she liked the silhouette very much, it was used as a template for the dress we created for her.

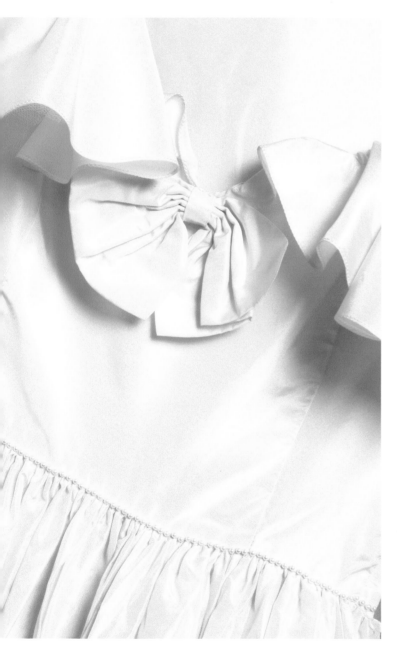

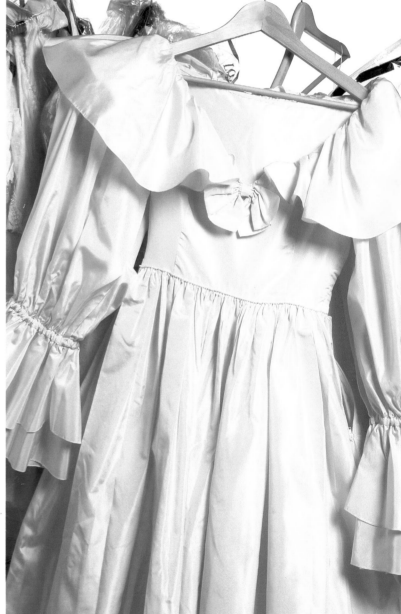

We did an enormous amount of research on other royal brides, and looked through as many books as we could find for inspiration and influence. One thing that immediately struck us was the use of antique lace in Queen Victoria's wedding dress, something that was already part of the Emanuel signature. We wanted to include as much lace as we could on the dress, and yet ensure a style that would suit a contemporary young royal bride.

Although Diana had mentioned a Spencer family tiara, we loved the romantic sense of the wax orange blossom bridal garland typical of the Victorian era. Elizabeth managed to find such a garland at Phillips, the auctioneers, but after working with it we discovered that it was too fussy, and so we quickly discarded the idea.

We were also curious to discover if there were certain emblems or motifs we should incorporate into the design, but none of the modern royal brides had used such ideas. There were no written instructions from the Palace, so we felt free to go back further in history, looking at the dresses of Princess Marie of Edinburgh, Princess Mary of Teck, and other designs from a more romantic era.

Another Emanuel signature idea that we wanted to include was the boned bodice to enhance Diana's shape (drawn in very tight at the waist). Also, we wanted to create a very full skirt to give a scale to the dress that would reflect the fact that the wedding was to be at St Paul's, one of the largest cathedrals in the world. In the back of our mind was the knowledge that Diana would arrive at the steps to St Paul's and so we researched royal trains. We discovered the longest train in history had been twenty-three feet. So we were very excited to think that we might create an even longer one, and the vision of what Diana would look like in the dress, climbing those steps.

Opposite We must have looked through dozens of paintings, photographs and engravings of royal brides, including those of Queen Victoria (left) and the first Lady Diana Spencer (right) seen here.

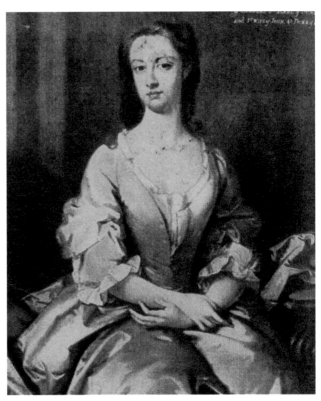

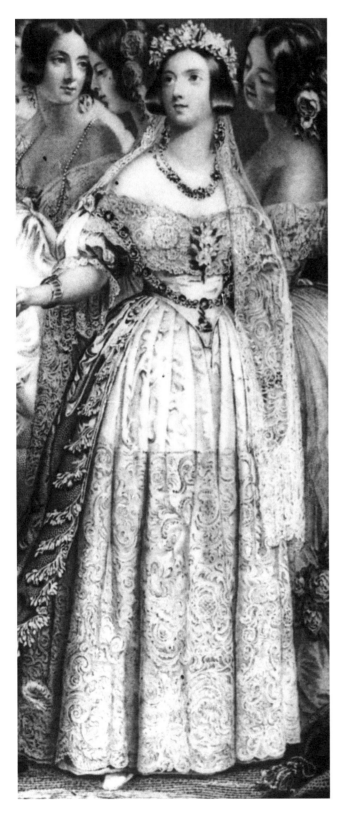

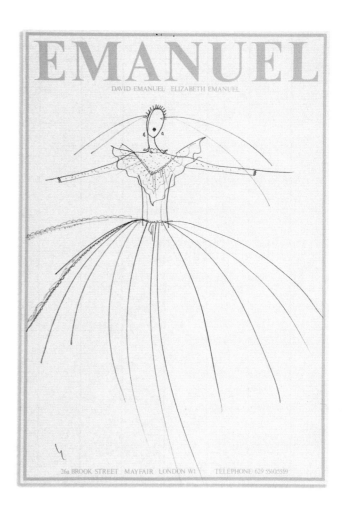

The day had finally arrived when we would present our designs for the wedding gown. A wary Diana and her mother, Mrs Shand Kydd, sat patiently on the showroom floor while we spread out our sketches around them. We have always had a problem with editing down our designs and, with the excitement of the prospect of creating the wedding gown of the century, our creative juices had really been flowing. The carpet was literally covered in our pencil drawings. It must have been quite a daunting sight for the future princess and her mother, who sat stunned and speechless for the first few minutes before they began to examine the sketches. We held our breath for what seemed like forever and then finally the smiles broke out.

Above, opposite, overleaf and pages 60–1 Some of the designs that were shown to Lady Diana and her mother were based on the dress on page 53, the silhouette of which Diana had liked. The final dress had elements from many of these designs. The big full sleeves, tight corseted bodice, puffball skirt and lots of frills and flounces were all typical of the New Romantic look of the early 1980s.

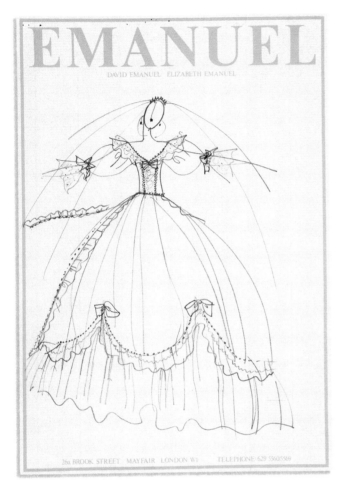

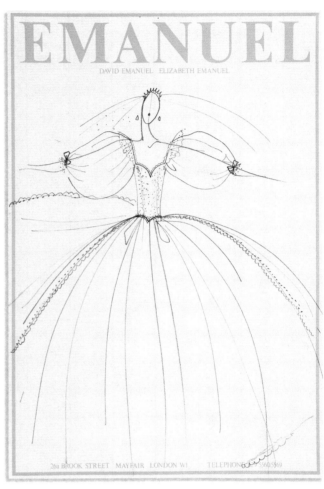

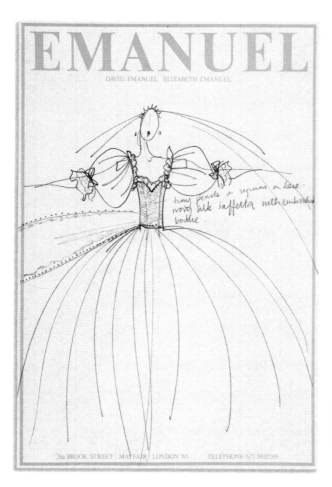

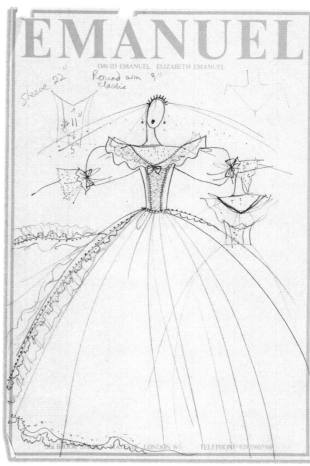

Above As well as sketches our process allowed Diana to try different bodice shapes, sleeves, and petticoats. At one session we asked her to throw on a huge petticoat over her jeans, for her to get used to the size and feel. Once she was comfortable, we then informed her that the final petticoat would be more than twice the size – she giggled with excitement.

Opposite This second choice of design was made as a back-up dress in case the secret of the real dress was discovered before the big day. The design was three-quarters complete and left hanging up in the studio. Fortunately it never had to be used.

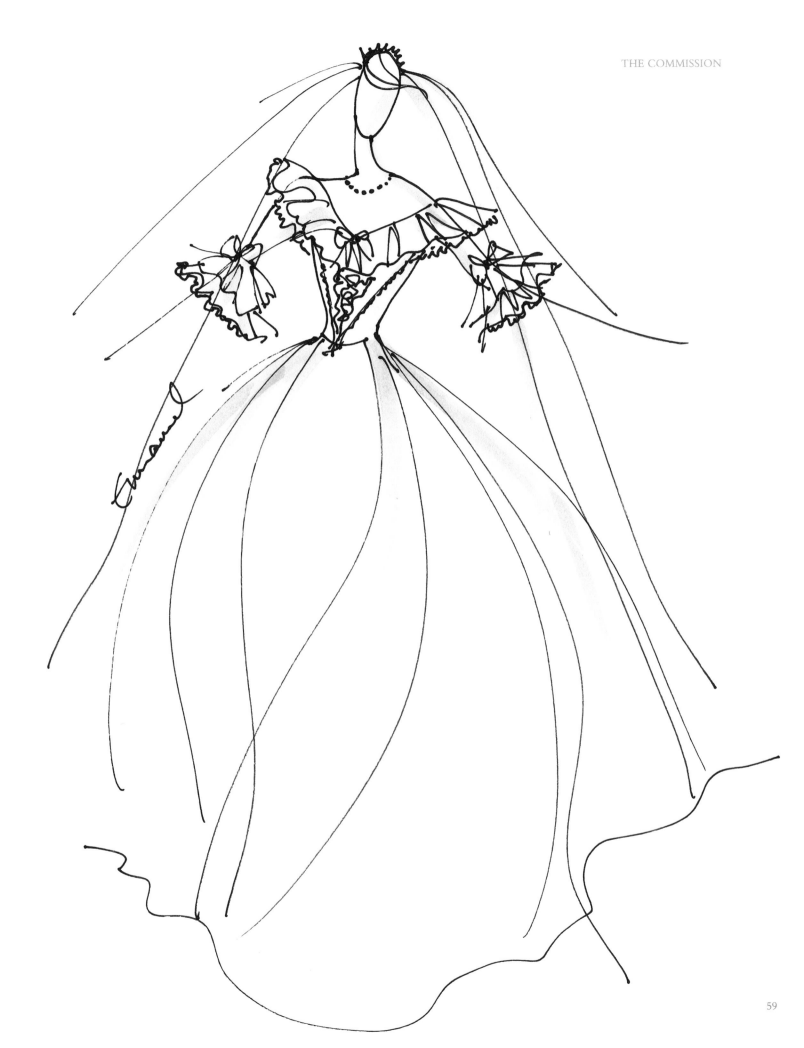

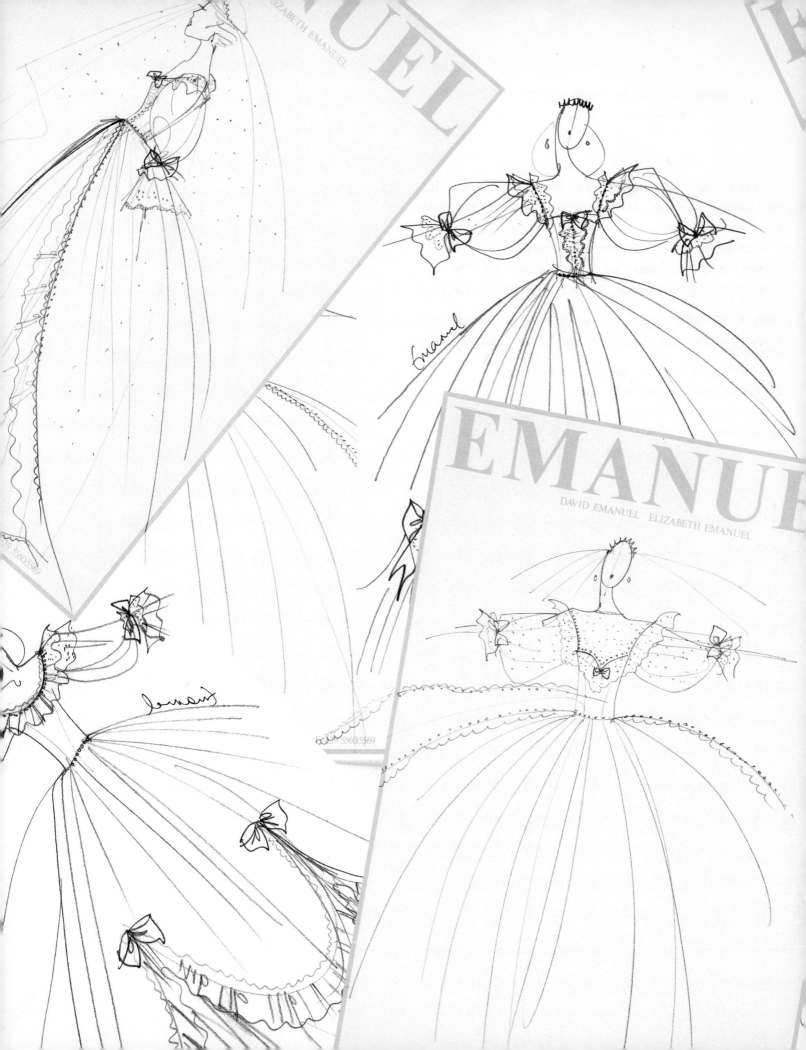

EMANUEL

DAVID EMANUEL   ELIZABETH EMANUEL

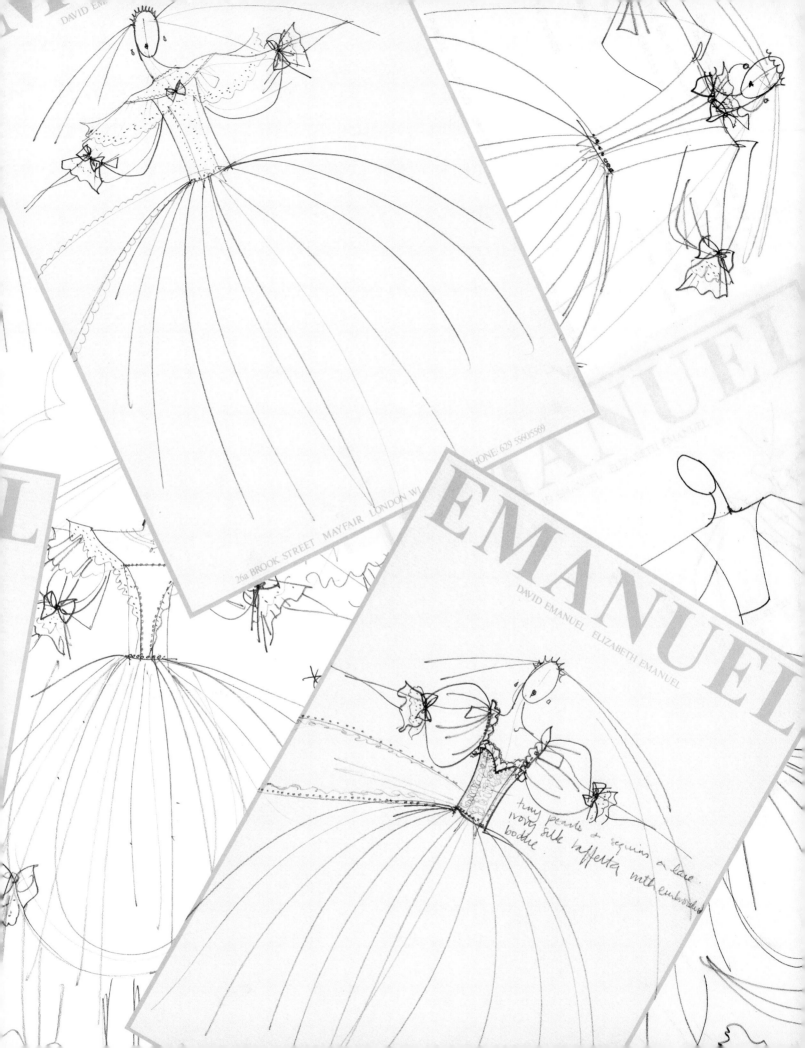

EMANUEL

DAVID EMANUEL ELIZABETH EMANUEL

tiny pearls & sequins & lace.
ivory silk taffeta withembroidered
bodice.

26a BROOK STREET MAYFAIR LONDON W1

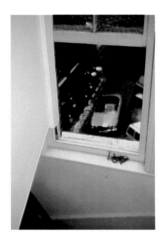 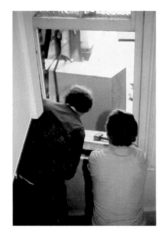 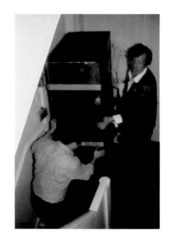 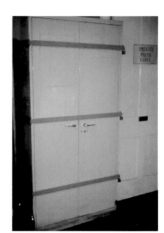

THE SAFE

As soon as we had begun to draw up sketches of possible designs for the dress, we realized that we would need to find somewhere secure in which to keep anything connected with it. We rang up a safe maker, who dutifully came and measured access to our little mews building. On the day the safe was due to be delivered, the truck backed up to the front door, only to find that the safe wouldn't fit through it.

The following day they returned and had to arrange for half a wall and a window to be taken out, and a huge crane was needed to hoist the safe into position. The press were beside themselves and it seemed that the whole of the West End could see what was happening. As the safe inched into its final position, we heard applause from the crowds outside – what we had wanted to be a very low-key event had turned into public entertainment. But every night from then on we kept everything to do with the dress locked securely in that safe.

Opposite For the purposes of security, we all had our pictures taken, though these identity cards were actually never used. The photograph shown top left is of our two security guards, Jim and Bert, who worked alternate nights to guard the safe.

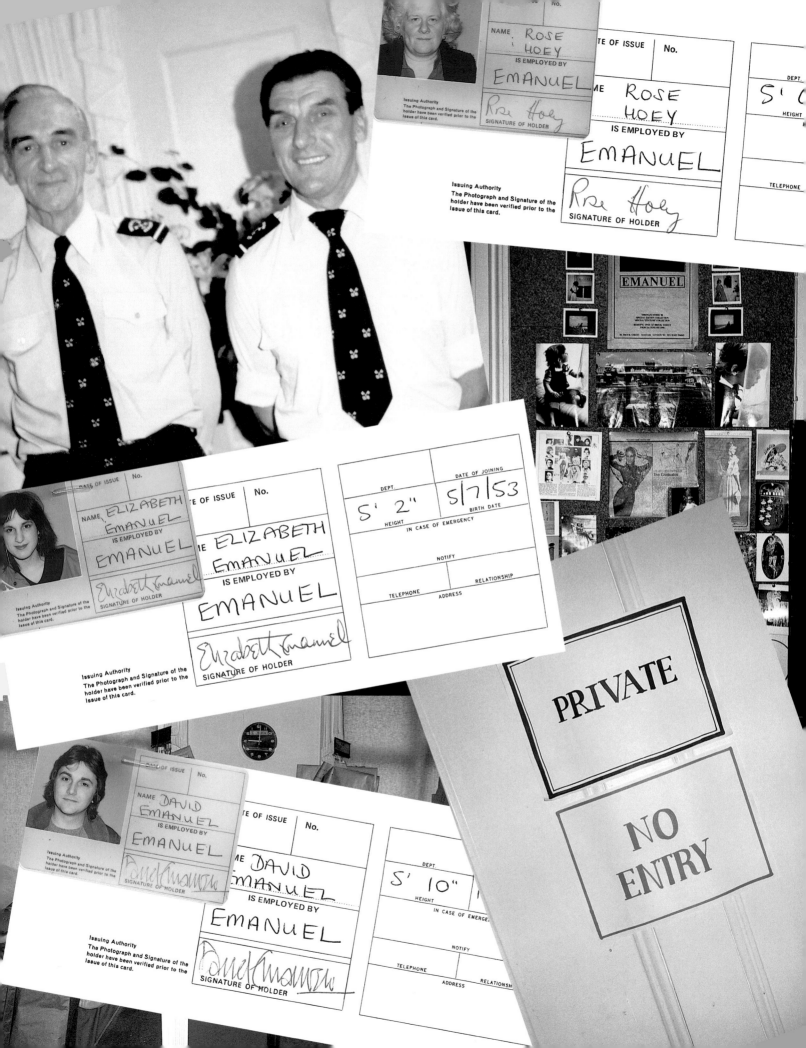

NAME ROSE HOEY
IS EMPLOYED BY
EMANUEL
Rose Hoey
SIGNATURE OF HOLDER

Issuing Authority
The Photograph and Signature of the
holder have been verified prior to the
issue of this card.

NAME ROSE HOEY
IS EMPLOYED BY
EMANUEL
Rose Hoey
SIGNATURE OF HOLDER

DEPT.
S'
HEIGHT
TELEPHONE

EMANUEL

NAME ELIZABETH EMANUEL
IS EMPLOYED BY
EMANUEL
Elizabeth Emanuel
SIGNATURE OF HOLDER

Issuing Authority
The Photograph and Signature of the
holder have been verified prior to the
issue of this card.

NAME ELIZABETH EMANUEL
IS EMPLOYED BY
EMANUEL
Elizabeth Emanuel
SIGNATURE OF HOLDER

Issuing Authority
The Photograph and Signature of the
holder have been verified prior to the
issue of this card.

DEPT.   DATE OF JOINING
S' 2"   5/7/53
HEIGHT   BIRTH DATE
IN CASE OF EMERGENCY
NOTIFY
TELEPHONE   RELATIONSHIP
               ADDRESS

NAME DAVID EMANUEL
IS EMPLOYED BY
EMANUEL
David Emanuel
SIGNATURE OF HOLDER

Issuing Authority
The Photograph and Signature of the
holder have been verified prior to the
issue of this card.

NAME DAVID EMANUEL
IS EMPLOYED BY
EMANUEL
David Emanuel
SIGNATURE OF HOLDER

Issuing Authority
The Photograph and Signature of the
holder have been verified prior to the
issue of this card.

DEPT.
S' 10"
HEIGHT
IN CASE OF EMERGENCY
NOTIFY
TELEPHONE
ADDRESS   RELATIONSH

PRIVATE

NO
ENTRY

"DIANA ALWAYS KNEW WHAT SHE LIKED. I THINK SHE FOUND IT TERRIBLY EXCITING. INITIALLY, IT WASN'T A WORLD SHE WAS WELL ACQUAINTED WITH. LIKE ANY YOUNG GIRL, SHE WAS MORE OF A T-SHIRT-AND-JEANS GIRL UP TO THAT POINT. I BELIEVE SHE WAS THRILLED BY THE WHOLE EXPERIENCE OF DESIGNER FASHIONS."

Felicity Clarke, former Beauty Editor of *Vogue*

Opposite Diana watches polo at Cowdray Park, 12 July 1981.
Sarah Ferguson can just be seen.

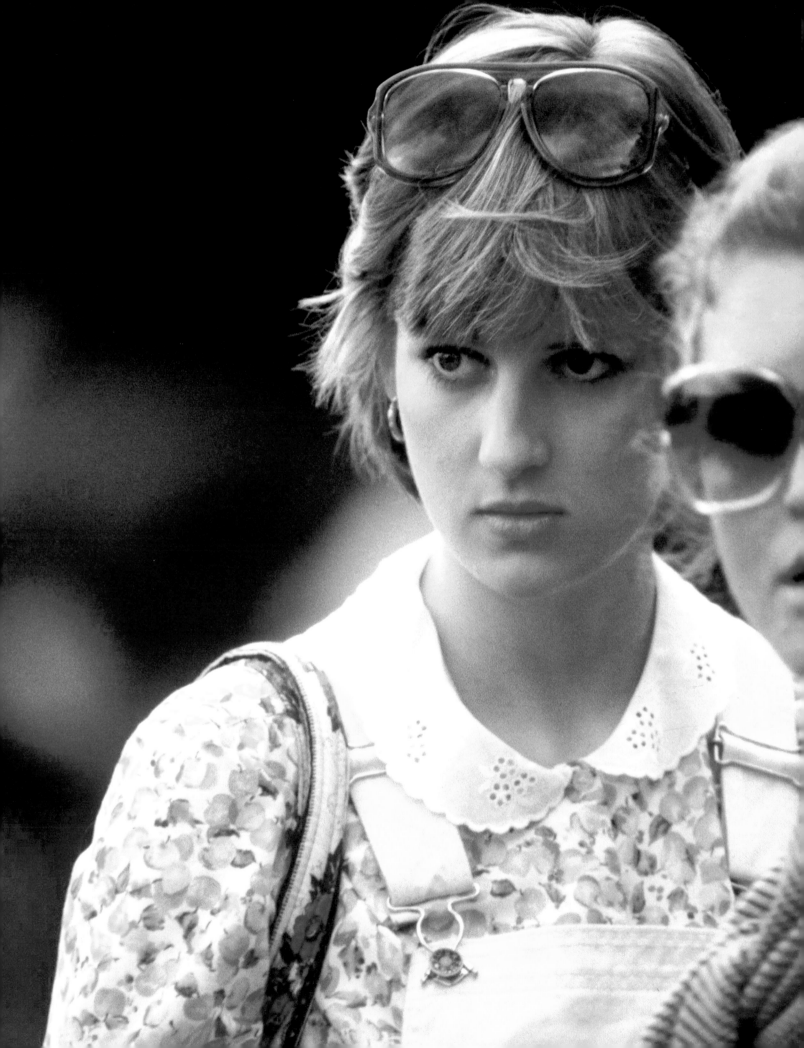

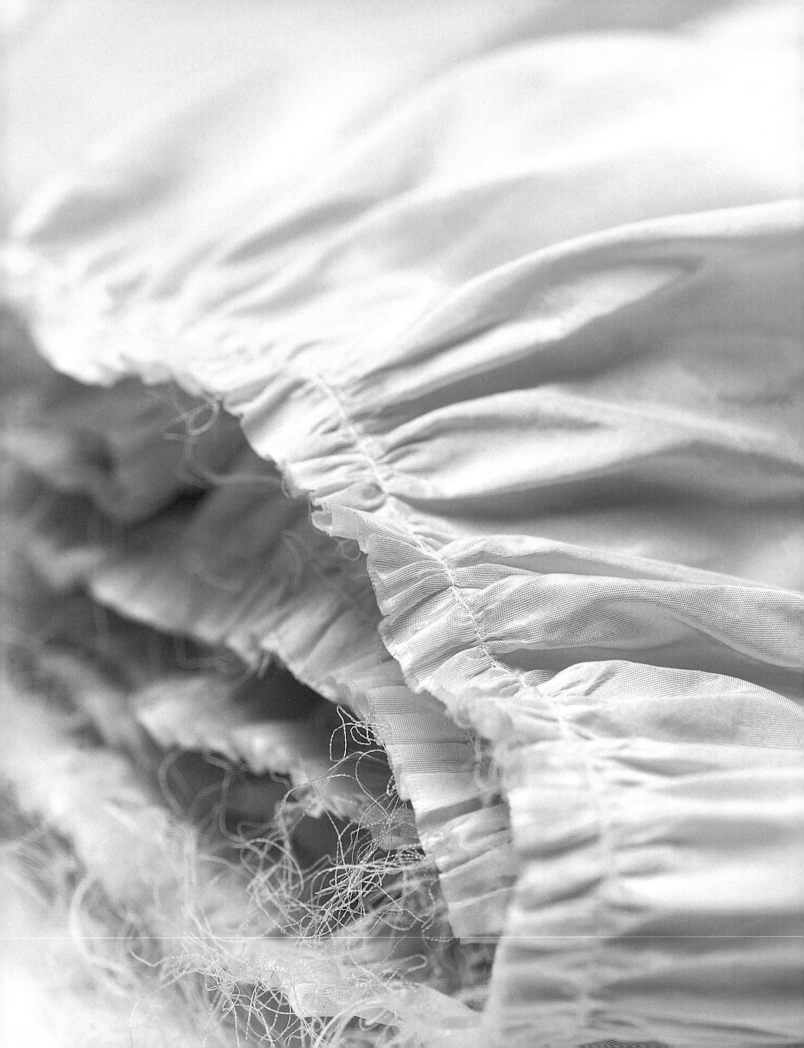

THE STUDIO

Once we had finalized the design of the wedding dress with Diana, we were ready to begin the lengthy process of actually creating it. But even before that stage we needed to source and order the very best materials. This took a large part of the three months we had left before the wedding.

With no instructions from the Palace – in theory we could have bought materials from anywhere in the world – we decided to try to make this, as far as possible, a British project. The huge press interest in the dress paid dividends for us here: we told them what we were trying to do and the result was that a lot of British manufacturers wrote to us. This enabled us to achieve our goal (although because the British silk worms at Lullingstone Silk Farm were not able to produce the quantity of silk we required for the weavers, they did have to import some raw silk).

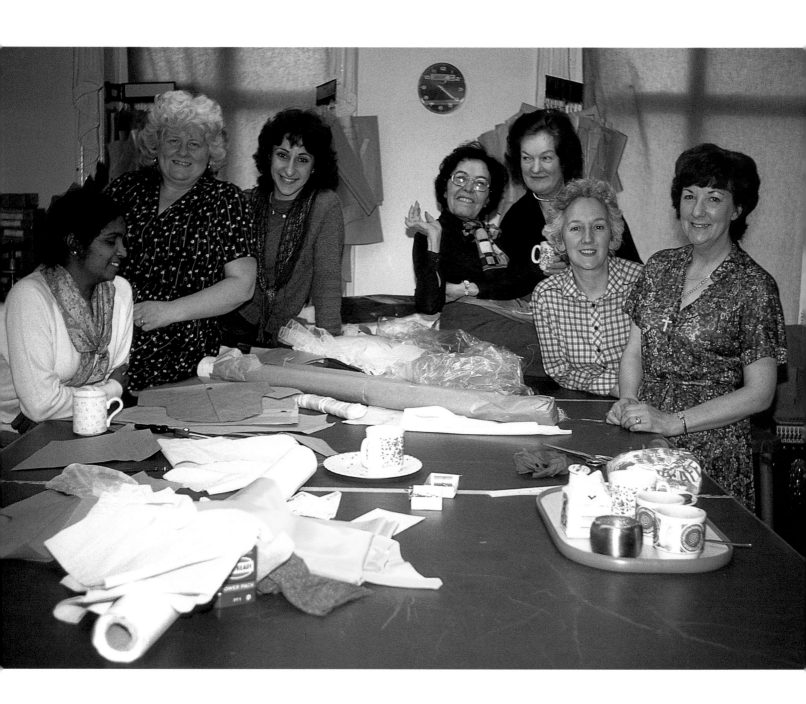

Above There is no way that we could ever have made that dress without our team of "Emanuel ladies". In addition to being very talented and hard working, they were extremely loyal and kept the dress a secret despite being offered huge sums of money by journalists hungry for a scoop. From left to right: Sarajana, Rose, Barbara, Nina, Rosaleen (Caroline's mum), Inez and Mildred.

THE TEAM

Every bride wants to keep her dress a secret until the wedding day, but with this royal wedding the need for secrecy was of the utmost importance. Our staff – our "Emanuel Ladies" as we called them – were highly trained women who were very faithful to us and we trusted them completely. Nevertheless, we decided that the fewer people who knew about the dress the better. We therefore hand-picked just two ladies to be in charged of the commission, while the other members of the team handled our other work. (In addition to making the royal wedding dress, we were also committed to completing orders for private clients at this time, as well as to creating a small collection that we would sell to the stores.) We tried to keep the team as tight as possible to ensure that the details of the dress were kept a secret, although as the important day drew nearer, we did need to recruit some additional help.

One of those we chose was Nina, who was our first seamstress and a wonderful lady. (She had come to us as a result of an advertisement we placed when we first started in business.) Nina was Greek and couldn't speak very good English and even when she started with us, was already quite elderly and slightly stooped with really long, bony hands – the result of many years of dressmaking. She was extremely meticulous and a real perfectionist and would work long hours hunched up over the sewing machine. The other main member of the team was Rose, another wonderful and very talented lady. Our PA, Caroline, who joined us at about this time, was also in on the secret.

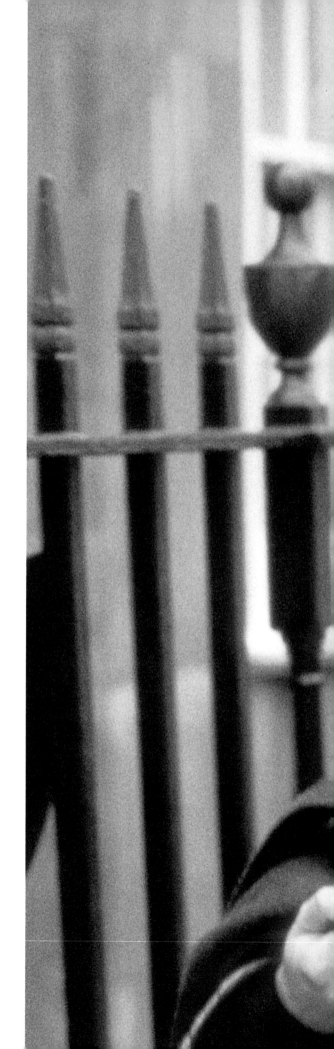

"Diana was very young at that time and she had no real idea about fashion. When we first met her she was wearing a little cardigan and a pie-crust-frilled blouse – very Sloane Ranger, very Knightsbridge – and had a short hairstyle. She was very shy and sweet, with quite a cherubic face. She would look at us coyly from under her thick fringe and blush frequently. Like most nineteen year-olds, she had never experienced a couture environment, so this was a totally new experience for her."

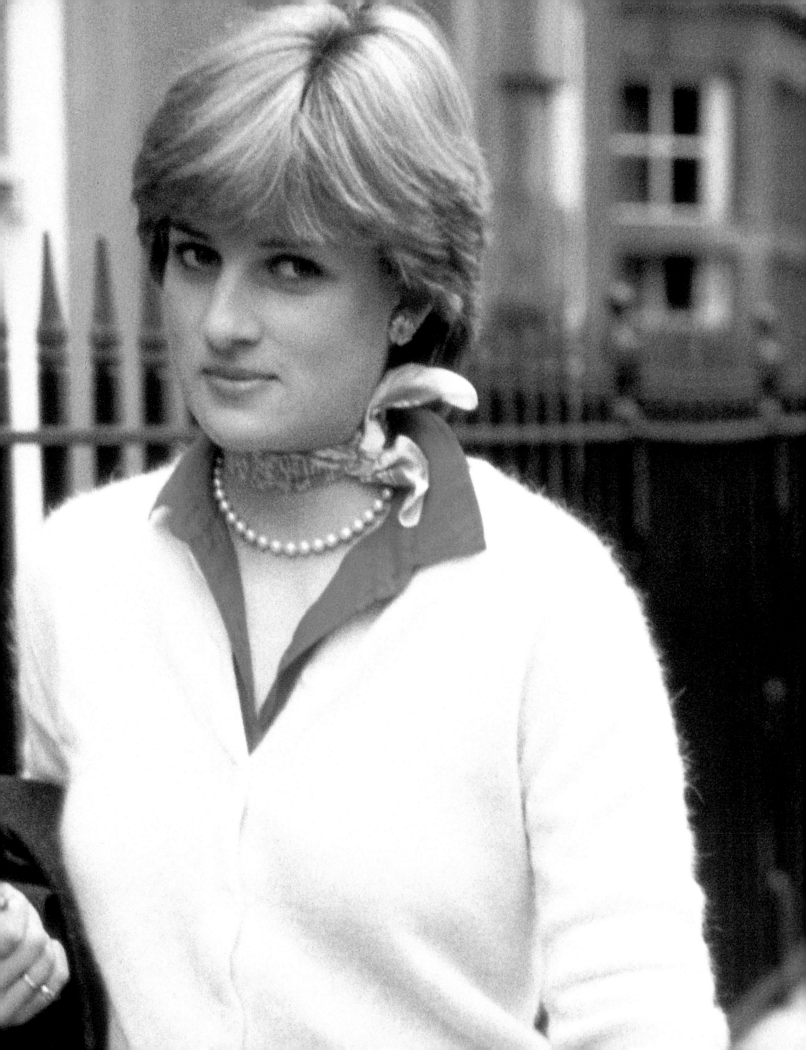

When clients attended appointments with us at our Brook Street studio, they would be buzzed through the front door, come up the first flight of stairs and enter through the double doors into the showroom. At the tiny little landing, concealed behind a draped curtain, were another three flights of stairs, which led to the workrooms and an office. All our clients only ever visited the showroom, but Diana was inquisitive and would constantly badger us to tell her what was upstairs. We explained to her that it was nothing exciting, but told her that the other floors were out of bounds to clients and that she could not go past the draped curtain.

On one particular day, David came back to the studio and rang the doorbell, but received no answer. Having found his key and let himself in, he then went up to the first-floor showroom. Although all the doors were open and petticoats were strewn about everywhere, there was no-one in sight. On the second floor, in the workroom and kitchen, he found most of the Emanuel ladies and our PA, Caroline, in tears, but no-one could explain what had happened. On the top floor he found Elizabeth with Nina and Rose, as usual – and with them was Diana. She had disobeyed our "No Entry" instructions in order to go and thank the team personally and individually for all the hard work they were putting into making her dress.

"Diana was very sweet and very generous. If she knew you'd worked really hard to do something for her, something special, she'd always write a little note to say thank you."

Opposite Controlled mayhem behind the scenes. The centre picture is of Elizabeth's mother, who happily volunteered to help with the embroidery, one of her personal passions. At the bottom is Nina, who was responsible for making the dress, which she called "her baby". It was hard work, but we all loved every minute of it.

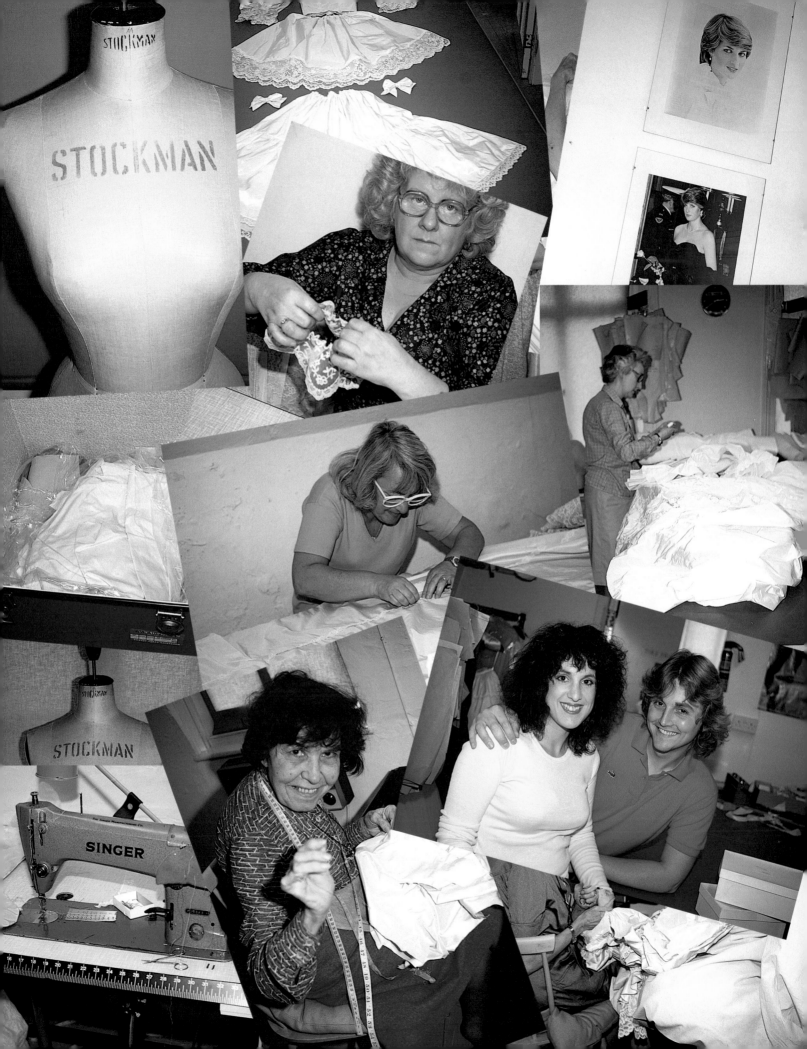

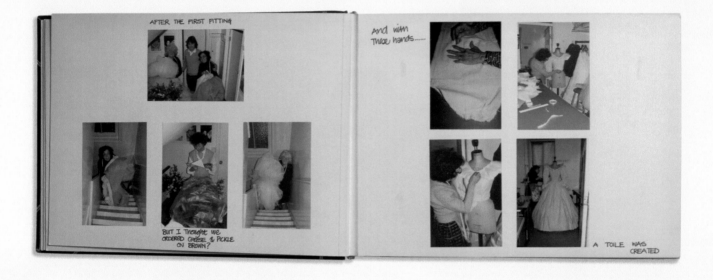

Above We decided to create our own records of events, and David took lots of photographs throughout the process of making the dress so that we could look back and remember every minute of it. We put a selection of them into a bound volume and presented it to the royal couple as a wedding gift so that they would know how much love and attention went into making her dress.
Opposite Nina's hands in action.

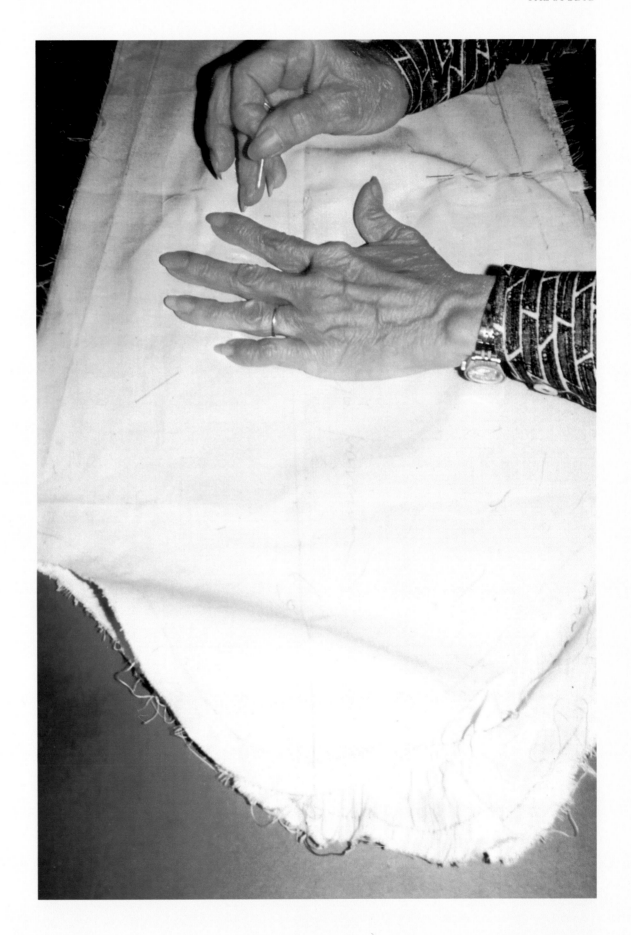

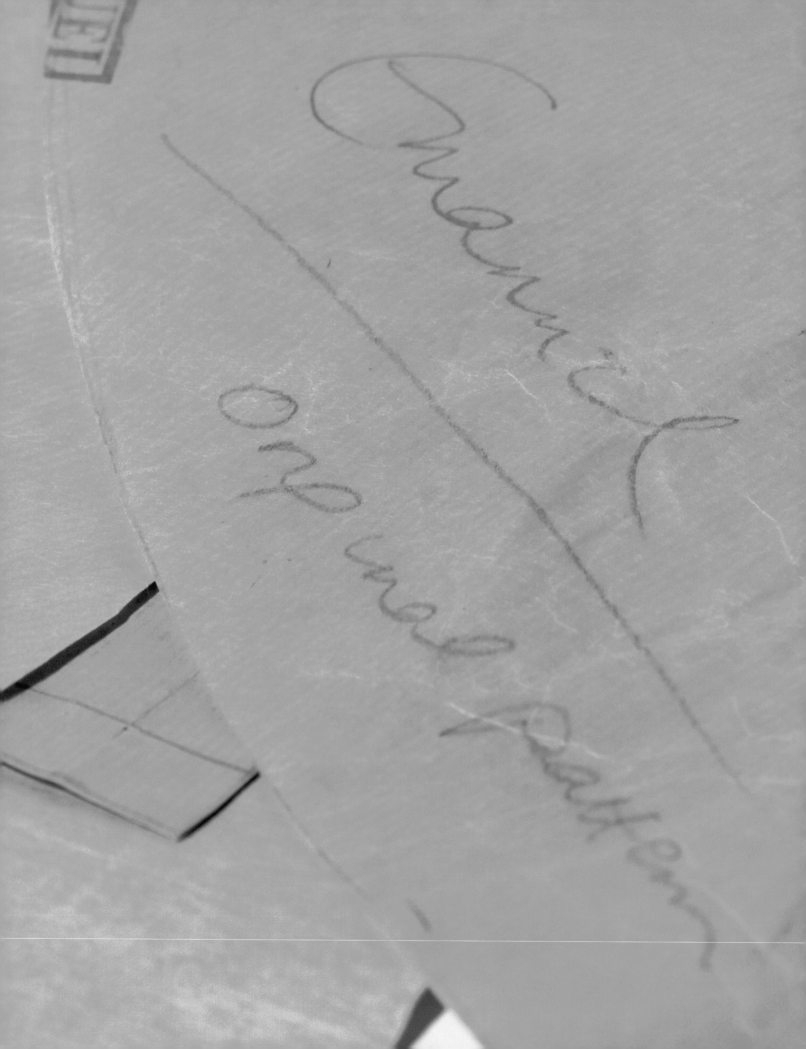

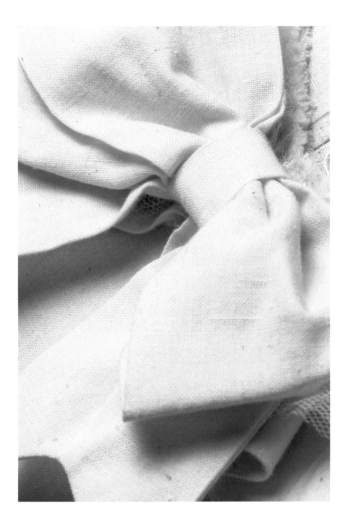
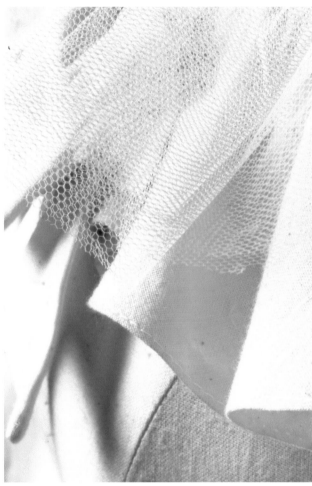

"Diana, like many nervous brides, must have lost about a stone and a half in weight during the run-up to the wedding, so we made lots of toiles, each bodice a size smaller."

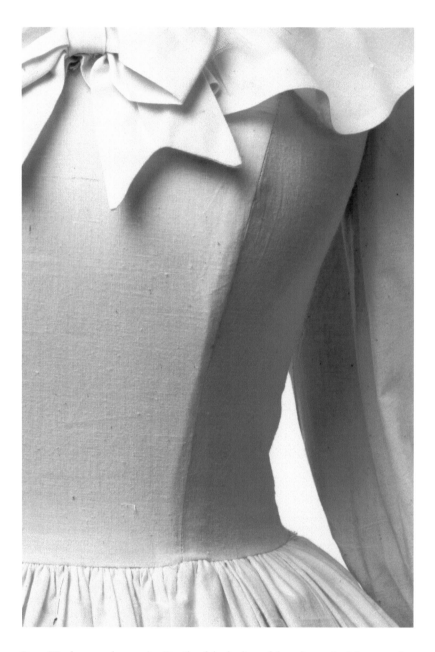

Page 77, above and opposite Details of the bodice of the calico toile. After several fittings, we ended up with a toile that was perfect, and it was then time for Nina to cut the dress out in the silk taffeta.

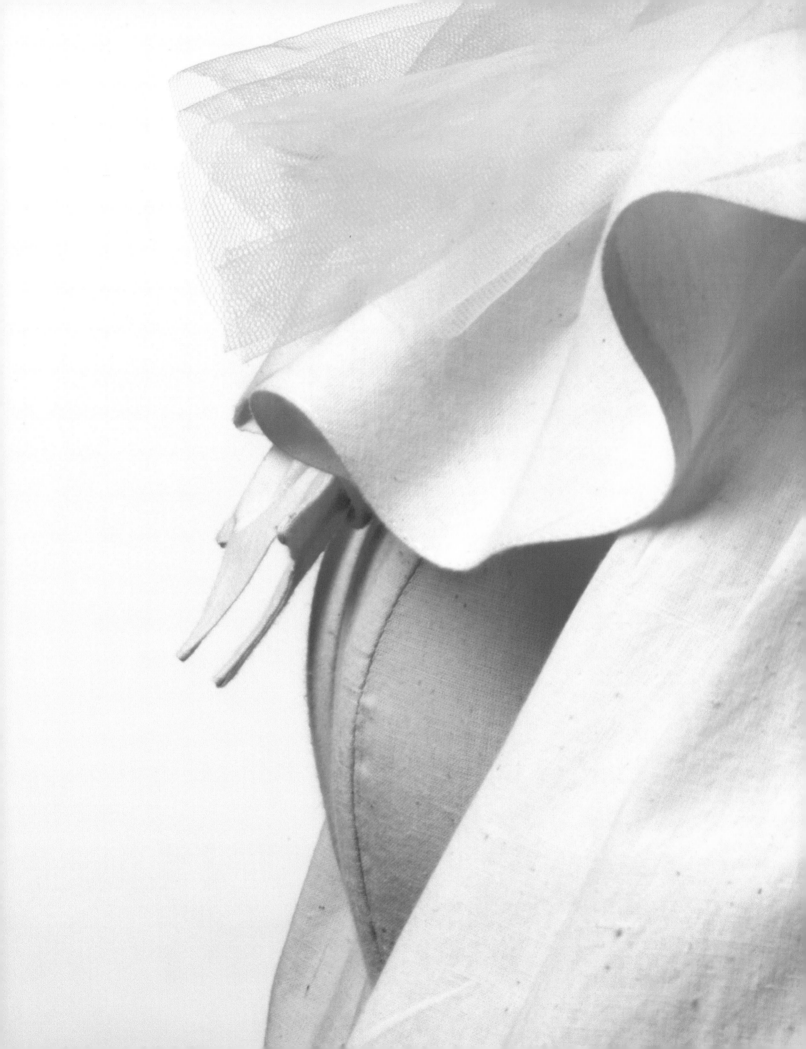

THE TOILES

The process of making a wedding dress is generally the same for every gown. You start with a sketch, then make a pattern. This pattern is then cut out in calico or another type of fabric to make a mock-up of the dress, which is called a toile. This enables you to make as many alterations as necessary before you finally transfer the corrections onto the patterns and cut into the actual silk.

We had to take the dress in several sizes and we didn't cut out the actual silk until the very last minute. We knew that once we started making the actual dress it was going to be very difficult to alter it – we had only had a limited amount of fabric and we didn't want to make any mistakes, to leave any pin marks or to have to start unpicking seams.

Each fitting was done by Nina, supported on occasion by Rose. Diana's fans seemed to have an uncanny knack of finding out when she would be coming in because a crowd would mysteriously appear outside our door. Then at the end of the fitting, Diana had to go out there, people would try to mob her. Even from those early days she was never really left alone.

Diana undoubtedly welcomed the brief respite that fittings at Brook Street would give her. Free for a while from the constant hounding by the paparazzi, she would always make time to chat with us over a cup of tea or coffee and would always ask after our children, Oliver and Eloise, who we brought in to the studio one day so that they could meet her.

Opposite A toile is a dressmaker's equivalent of a working document, used to ensure the final dress is the perfect fit.

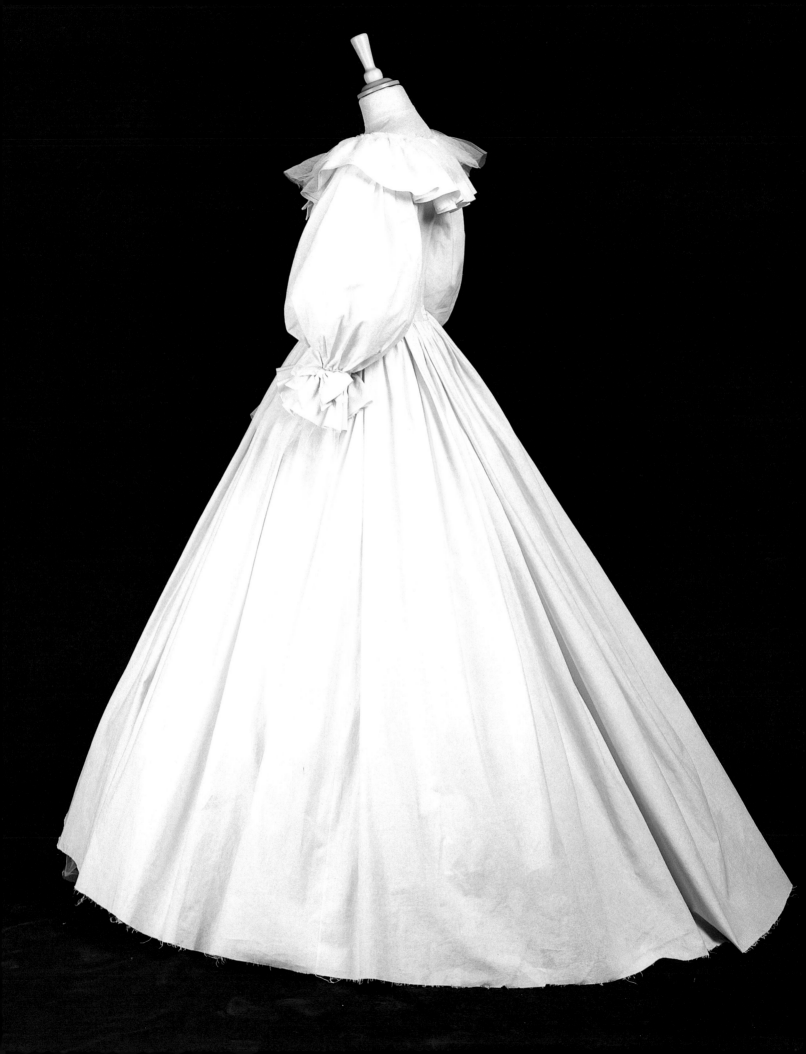

THE SILK

While we were trying to source British materials, we were surprised to discover that there was a silk farm in England: Lullingstone Silk Farm in Dorset. We would have loved to use their British silkworms to supply all the silk for the dress, but unfortunately, there just weren't enough of them to produce the quantity of silk that we were going to need. Nevertheless, they did manage to produce enough silk to include in the veil.

We undertook extensive research, and took advice from *Vogue*, to find the best weavers of silk taffeta. We wanted to have a very special taffeta that nobody else could ever duplicate. Eventually we decided on Stephen Walters, a small, well-established company, which is based in Sudbury, Suffolk. Founded in the eighteenth century, it is the oldest silk weavers in Britain.

Opposite The beautiful silk tafetta used in the dress was ordered in two colourways, white and ivory, so that not even the silk weavers would know what shade the dress was going to be.

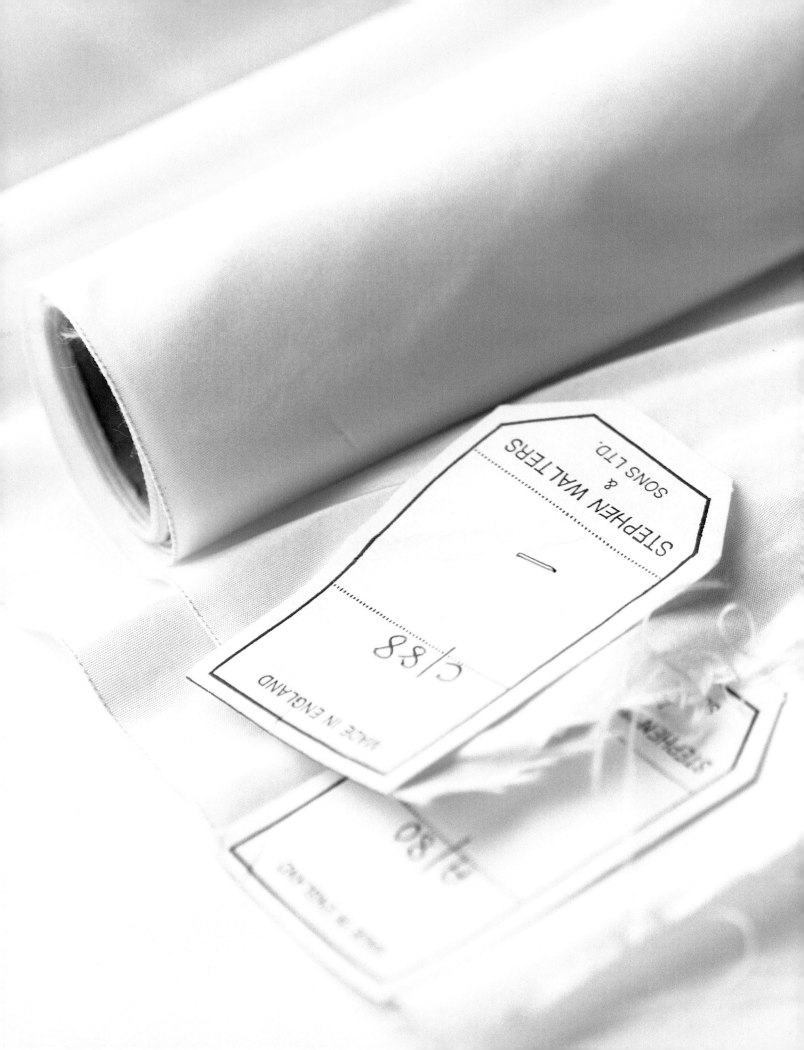

Stephen Walters & Sons Limited

SUDBURY SILK MILLS
SUDBURY · SUFFOLK · CO10 6XB
ENGLAND

Telephones:
SUDBURY (0787) - 72266

Telex:
987881

Telegrams:
WALTERS, SUDBURY-SUFFOLK.

PBW/jmm.   11th March, 1981.

Emanuel,
26 Brook Street,
London W.1.

Dear Sirs,

    We have been delighted to learn from the Times
that you are to design the Wedding dress for Lady Diana
Spencer. We expect for this very special occasion you
will be considering real Silk, and would like to hope the
fabric will be woven in this country.

    As established Silk weavers we are able to offer
fabrics in Silk specially designed and woven to order, and
would be confident of being able to produce a material
exactly to your own detailed requirements. We would be
grateful for an opportunity to show you some of the things
we have made, and would be happy to call on you at any
time to suit your convenience.

    If we can be of assistance will you please
telephone us, asking for David or Peter Walters.

       Yours faithfully,
    STEPHEN WALTERS & SONS LTD.

Mr. Linton

P.S.
    We did have the honour of weaving the Silk for
Princess Anne's Wedding dress, the material designed and
produced specially for the occasion.

"WE WERE DELIGHTED TO BE CHOSEN TO WEAVE THE SILK FOR LADY DIANA'S WEDDING DRESS. AS THE EIGHT GENERATION OF MY FAMILY TO RUN THE BUSINESS, IT IS A SOURCE OF IMMENSE PRIDE TO HAVE PERSONALLY BEEN A PART OF SUCH A HISTORIC EVENT, JUST AS IT HAD BEEN TO PREVIOUS GENERATIONS OF THE FAMILY WHO HAD WOVEN SILK FOR THE CORONATION GOWN OF QUEEN ELIZABETH II AND THE WEDDING DRESS OF PRINCESS ANNE."

David Walters, chairman of Stephen Walters & Sons Limited

David Walters, the head of the family firm, wrote to us when he first heard of our appointment to design the royal wedding dress and asked to be considered to weave the silk. The company has a long-established tradition in weaving silk for the Royal family, having woven the silk lining for Queen Elizabeth II's coronation gown and also the silk for the wedding dress of Princess Anne. (The company also supplied the silk that was used to make the gowns worn by Deborah Kerr in the film *The King and I*.)

A few days later, we wrote to David requesting a meeting and he came in to see us at Brook Street, bringing with him various samples of beautiful silks in different colours and weights. After much discussion, we requested a heavier weight of taffeta, which would have to be specially woven to our requirements. This would help create the distinctive shape of the final dress.

As at every stage of making the dress, we were very conscious of security. We didn't want anyone to find out what we were doing, so after they had made us some one-metre samples in different colours, we ordered lengths of fabric in white and ivory – the shade that we eventually used in Diana's gown – so that nobody would know which we were going to use.

The mill at Glemsford twisted the raw silk and dyed it to the specially chosen colour to match the lace. These were one-off colours that were never used for anything else. The shoe satin was also sent to Glemsford for dying to ensure a perfect match to the dress material. The warp was twisted as two-ply and the weft as twelve-ply and the warp consisted of nearly 11,000 strands, each one individually attached by hand to the loom.

Above right Some of the gorgeous samples of silk David Walters showed us. In the end we decided to use a classic ivory.

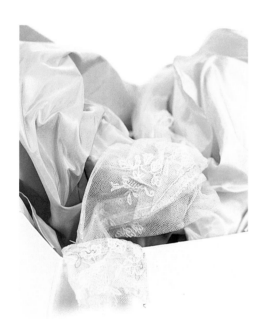

Two forty-one-metre lengths were woven; the additional one, woven in case of accidents, was subsequently used for the Madame Tussauds dress. The loom was stripped down and rebuilt especially for the weaving, and at a rate of about one metre per hour, the weaving of each bolt took nearly a full working week. Mr Lynton, the head weaver at the mill, supervised the actual weaving process and met with us to deliver the finished bolts of silk.

Thankfully, perhaps helped by the fact that Stephen Walters is a family-run firm, they ensured complete discretion throughout. Employees were never told the real purpose of the special job, and though various members were approached by the press, no-one betrayed the secret.

The true significance of what we'd been commissioned to produce dawned on us only gradually, and we had no idea at first how intrusive the press attention and speculation surrounding the dress would become. But we soon realized that it helps to have a sense of humour in such a stressful situation and we resolved to do our best to outwit the press and to have fun doing so. Nobody would ever guess!

One of our tricks was to attach bits of coloured thread to our clothing or to leave one or two outside our front door. Inevitably some-one would pick up a pink or blue thread and a whole new set of rumours would start. We also used to throw out fake scraps of fabric because we knew that people would be rifling through our bins. In addition, we were careful to ensure that no arrangements made were ever the same. We tried to arrive at a different time each day, just to keep the press on their toes. This subterfuge clearly worked as one of the newspapers even ran the headline, "Will Diana Wed in Pink?"

CUTTING THE SILK

Once we had taken delivery of the finished bolts of silk, we were keen to see how the fabric would make up. So we decided to experiment on the bodice shape, and made up a sample. This enabled us to see how the fabric would behave when stitched and pressed, and also canvassed, lined and finally boned. Through experience, we knew that some fabrics look and feel better on the sample swatch than they do when made up into gowns. Fortunately this material lived up to all our expectations – a huge relief, and from that point on we knew it would look wonderful as a finished dress.

Opposite One of the first sample bodices from an early fitting.

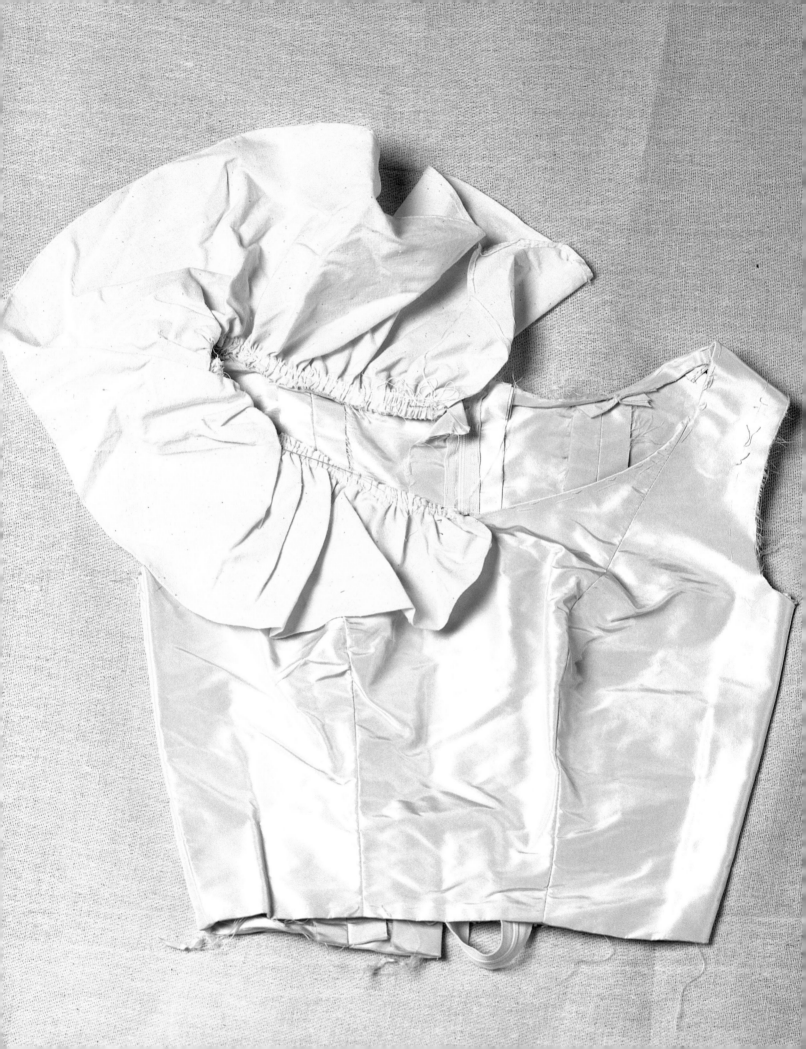

"When it came to cutting the silk, Nina had to have complete control. Nobody dared venture upstairs to the attic where she was working. She would spend hours positioning everything, getting it all right, making sure the fabric was absolutely straight, that it wasn't going to move. But once the fabric was cut out, we knew the dress was finally on the road – it was all starting to happen."

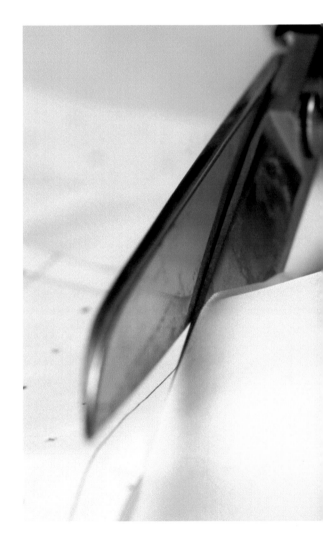

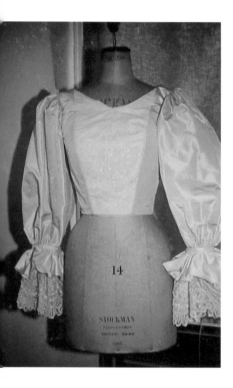
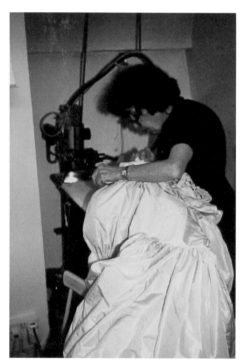
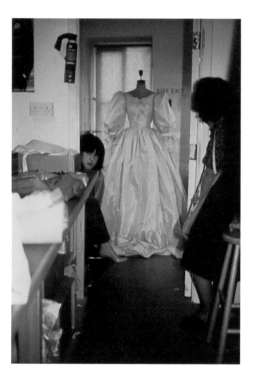

Above and opposite Nina at work on the dress. She was a master of detail and a real perfectionist. The picture on the right shows her working on the beautiful lace flounces on the sleeve and on the pearl detail.

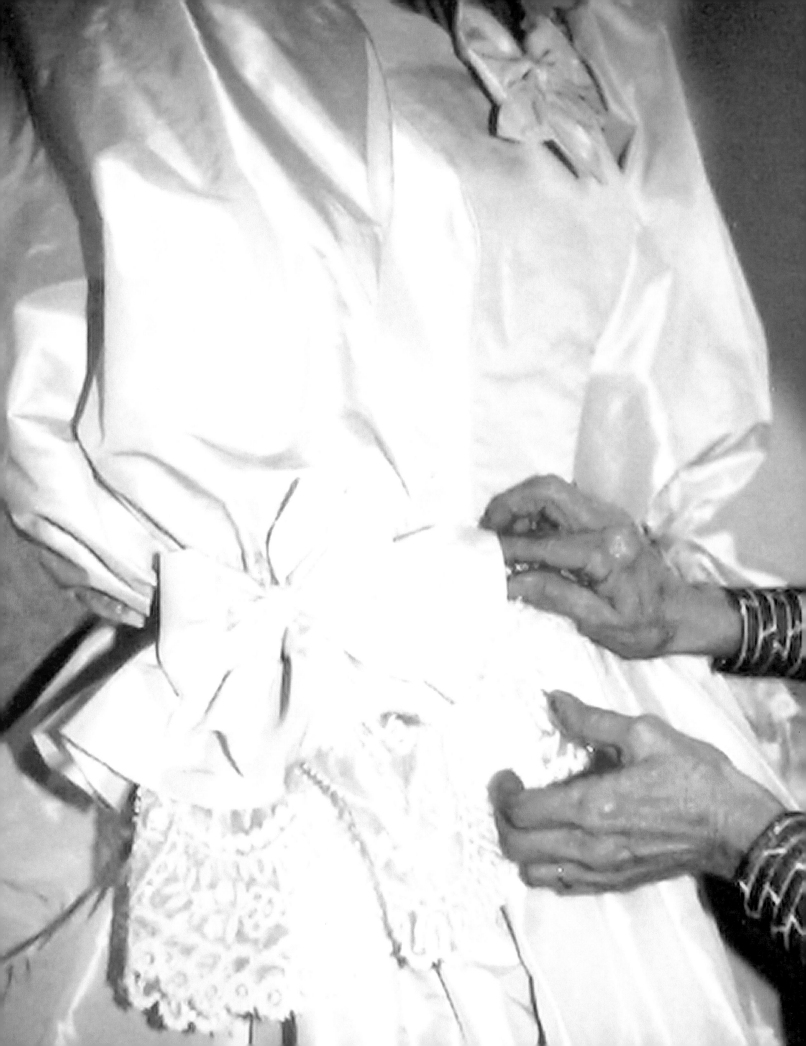

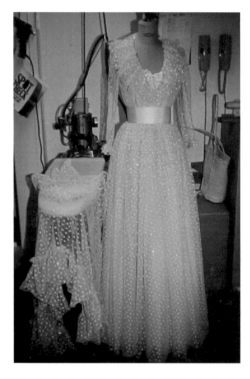

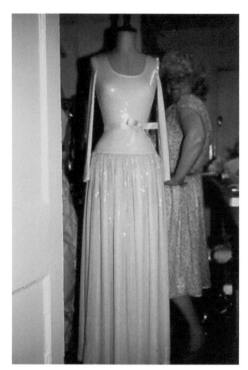

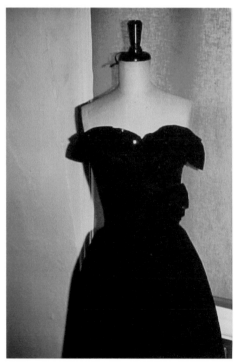

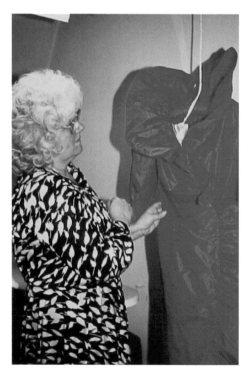

MORE DRESSES
FOR DIANA

Throughout this period, and indeed after the wedding, Diana also asked us to design several other dresses for her ever increasing public diary of engagements. This allowed us to have free reign with colour and silhouette, a welcome variation from our work on the bridal gown.

After each such engagement, every detail of each dress was increasingly scrutinised by editors of newspapers, magazines and even television correspondents. With each passing week, the momentum built, and the press scrutiny intensified. This added to the already substantial levels of pressure we felt, but served as good rehearsal for the months ahead.

Diana even brought us back the now infamous black dress to be re-modelled to her new slimmer size and shape. In fact, the alterations were to be so extensive that we ended up making a completely new dress.

Opposite Some of the other dresses that we made for Diana during the period, including: (top left) a pale blue net dress, spangled with mother of pearl sequins and a pink satin sash, which was worn for the state visit of the King of Saudi Arabia, (top right) a pale peach stretch satin and matching sequin spangled toile dress worn on several occasions including the royal gala of the musical *Starlight Express*, (bottom left) the second incarnation of the infamous black dress, (bottom right) the shocking pink silk taffeta dress worn at the pre-wedding ball at Buckingham Palace.

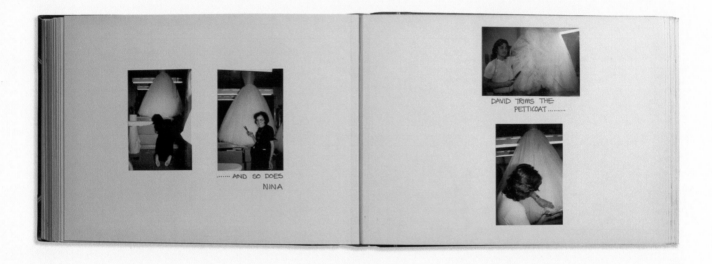

.......AND SO DOES
NINA

DAVID TRIMS THE
PETTICOAT.........

Above and opposite More pictures from the photograph album. The petticoats seemed to grow over time. There were at least fifty metres of net in a single petticoat. Trimming them was rather like giving someone a haircut.

Overleaf, left This petticoat was made to be worn under the toile for fittings and was used for the dress rehearsal at St. Paul's and at the Royal Mews, where Diana practised getting in and out of the coach to see how the dress would handle on the day.
Overleaf, right Made in case Diana spilt something down herself on the day, this overskirt could be fitted over the top of the real one if needed. Thankfully, it wasn't!

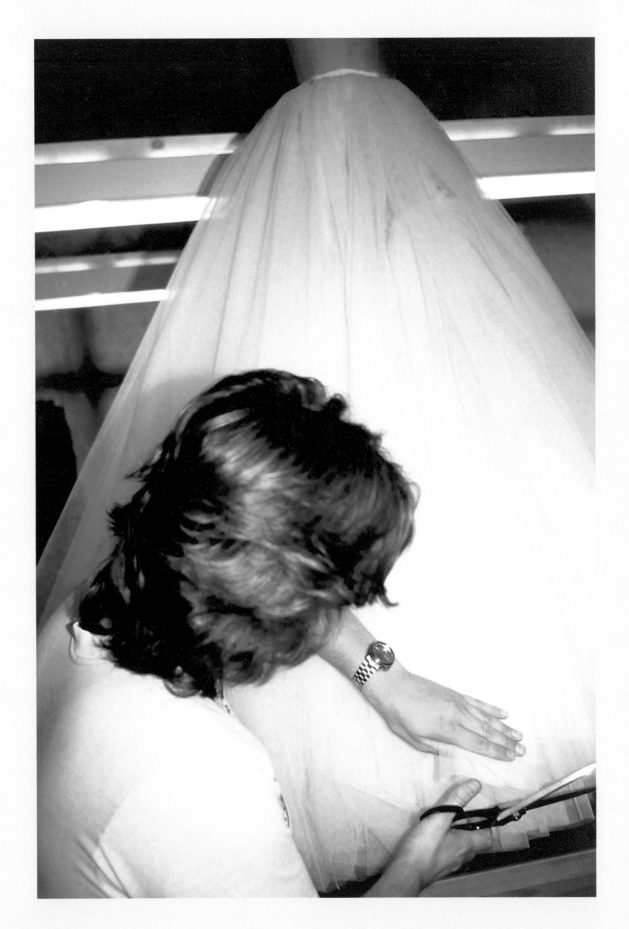

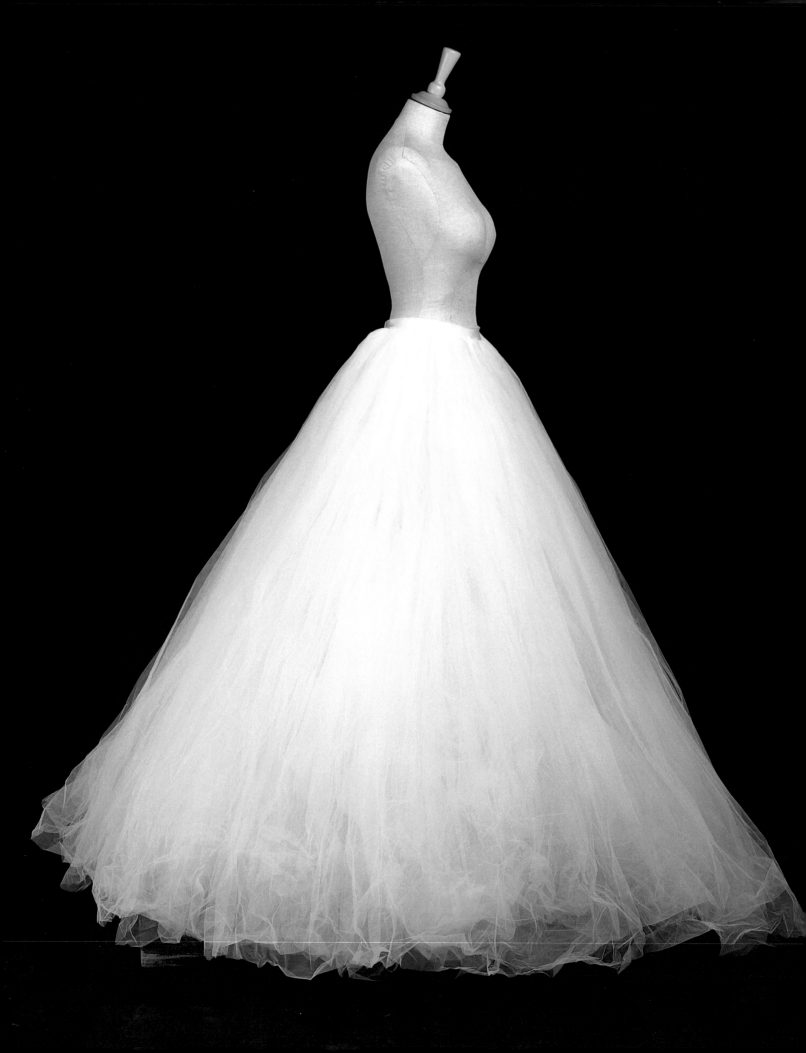

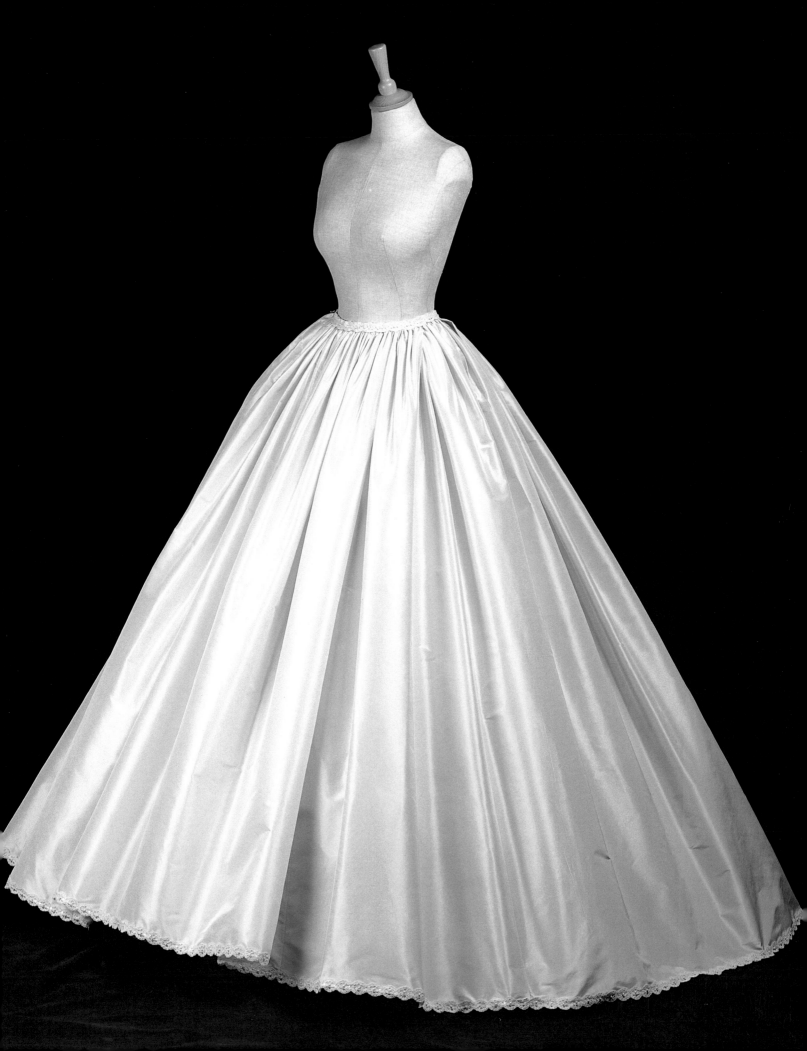

"As we continued to work on our labour of love in the studio, it had never even occurred to us that we would be formally invited to be among the 2,500 guests to attend the actual marriage service in St Paul's. Imagine our surprise when one day's post brought a heavily padded envelope bearing the Buckingham Palace crest, with our address handwritten in the most beautiful calligraphy. Inside was our personal invitation. The excitement was overwhelming, until Elizabeth exclaimed, 'What am I going to wear. I don't want to wear a hat!'

Typically Diana had touchingly thought of us, but her generosity of spirit didn't end there. Nina, Rose and Caroline were also invited. Suddenly everybody needed a new frock!"

*The Master of the Household
is commanded by Her Majesty to invite*

Mr and Mrs David Emanuel

*to a Reception at Buckingham Palace
to be given by The Queen and The Duke of Edinburgh
on Monday, 27th July, 1981
before the Marriage of His Royal Highness
The Prince of Wales to the Lady Diana Spencer*

*A reply is requested to
The Master of the Household, Buckingham Palace
To reduce traffic congestion please arrive
between 10.00 p.m. and 10.15 p.m.*

*White Tie
or
Black Tie*

Decorations

*The Lord Chamberlain is Commanded by
The Queen and The Duke of Edinburgh to invite*

Mr and Mrs D. Emanuel

to the Marriage of

His Royal Highness The Prince of Wales

with

*The Lady Diana Spencer
in St. Paul's Cathedral
on Wednesday, 29th July, 1981 at 11.00 a.m.*

*An answer is requested to the Lord Chamberlain,
St. James's Palace, London, S.W.1.*

*Dress: Uniform, Morning Dress
or Lounge Suit.*

THE BRIDESMAIDS

The announcement of who would be attending Diana as her bridesmaids was given while we were in the process of making the wedding dress. There were going to be five girls: Lady Sarah Armstrong-Jones, the daughter of HRH Princess Margaret, was the eldest at seventeen years old and was to be head bridesmaid. Next in line were India Hicks, Prince Charles' goddaughter, who was thirteen, and Sarah Jane Gaselee (eleven). The two youngest were Catherine Cameron (six, another of Prince Charles' goddaughters) and little Clementine Hambro, a petite blonde girl of five years old who had been a pupil at the Young England Kindergarten, where Lady Diana worked. (There were also two page boys: Edward Van Cutsem and Lord Nicholas Windsor, eight and seven years old respectively.)

Inspired in part by an old painting she had seen of a little girl, Elizabeth had already been doodling – something she does a lot when she's talking on the phone – and gradually ideas for these bridesmaids dresses began to take shape. As we had done for her own dress, we showed Diana lots and lots of sketches, and she loved them all. Then it was just a question of editing them down.

Although we wanted to keep the style of all the bridesmaids' dresses romantic, historical and very pretty –

Above This note from Lady Sarah Armstrong-Jones, sent to us after the wedding, echoes the sentiments of the other, younger bridesmaids, who also seemed delighted with their dresses.
Opposite Sent to Elizabeth on a postcard, this illustration was the original insspiration for the bridesmaids' dresses. Overlaying it are samples of the silk and lace used in the dresses.

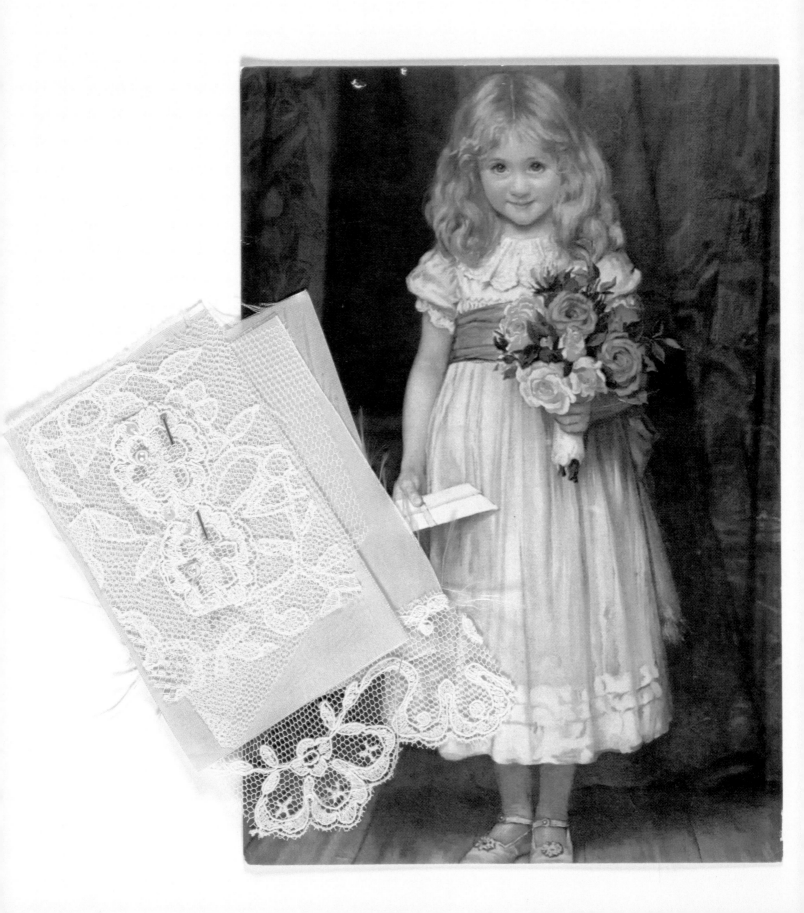

like Diana's own wedding gown – we were also keen to make the bridesmaids a bit different from each other, as was appropriate for their different ages. We knew that Clementine and Catherine, as the youngest, would look really cute, so we designed Victorian flower-girl dresses – all very flouncy and frilly – for them. The dress we made for Sarah Armstrong-Jones, on the other had, was more streamlined, more grown-up. All five dresses were of exactly the same colour silk as Diana's gown, but of a lighter weight, and each of the bridesmaids also wore a beautiful gold sash and matching shoes, the colour inspired by the Mountbatten rose.

Elizabeth had seen a painting of a little girl carrying a basket of flowers that was very pretty and slightly old-fashioned – just the look we were wanting to create. So we asked Edward Goodyear, who was responsible for the flowers for the bridesmaids, to create little flower baskets rather than posies for them to carry, which looked very romantic. The younger four girls also wore flower circlets.

Opposite Samples of the gold silk, also supplied by Stephen Walters, that were used for sashes for the bridesmaids' dresses.

Bridesmaids dresses with boned, fitted bodices
full, ruffled skirts worn with net petticoats.

Trimmed with old lace, tiny pearls and tiny
sequins.

Sash and bows in old gold pure silk taffe

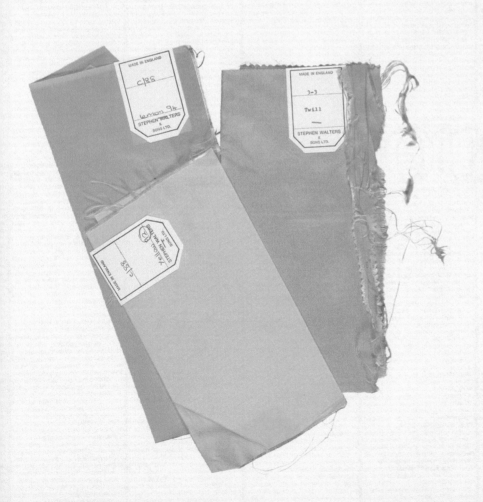

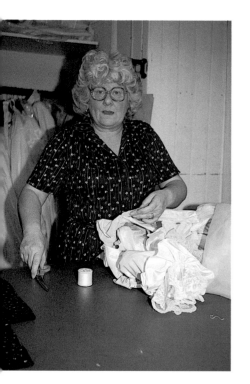 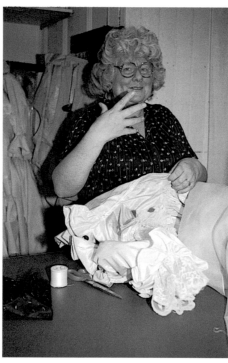 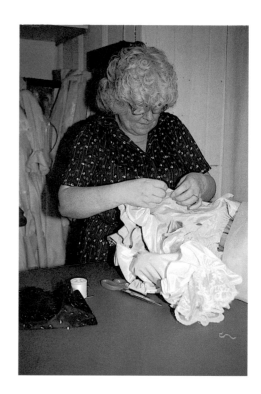

"DIANA ... SHE WAS SUCH A WONDERFUL LADY — SO DOWN TO EARTH.
I REMEMBER ONCE AT BUCKINGHAM PALACE SAYING TO HER THAT IT WAS
AMAZING TO THINK I WAS ON THE INSIDE, HAVING STOOD OUTSIDE AS
A TOURIST SO MANY TIMES. SHE LAUGHED AND SAID WE SHOULD
GO OUT ONTO THE BALCONY AND WAVE AT ALL THE PEOPLE OUTSIDE —
AND WE DID!"

Rose Hoey

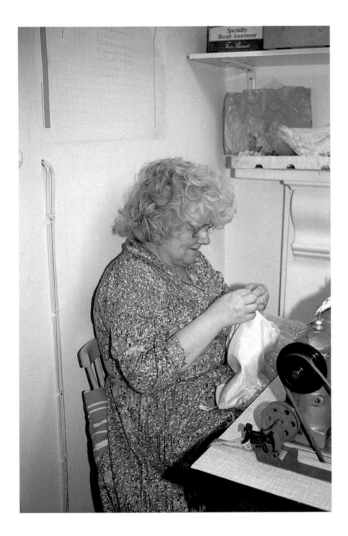

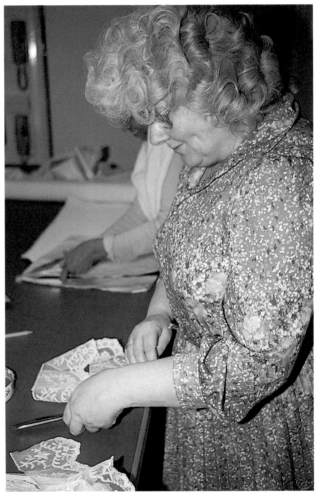

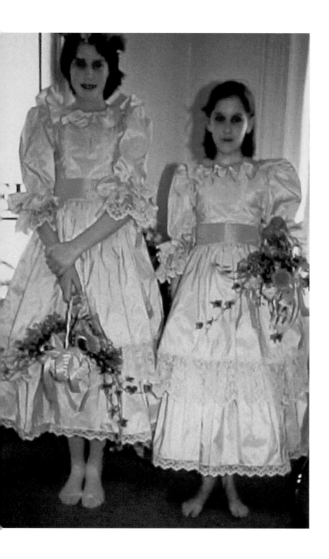

Left India Hicks (left) and Sarah Jane Gaselee (right) wearing their final dresses and trying out prototype flower baskets in the studio at Brook Street.
Opposite A rough sketch of the dress we designed for India and Sarah Jane. Their dresses were identical in style, as were those worn by the youngest two bridemaids, Clementine and Catherine.

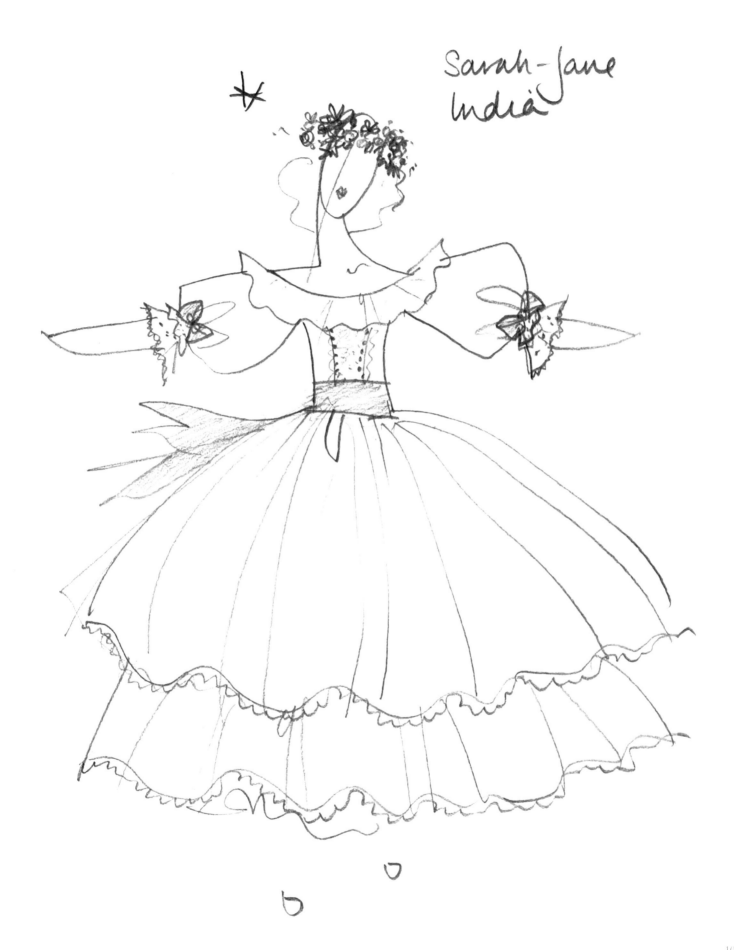

Sarah-Jane
India

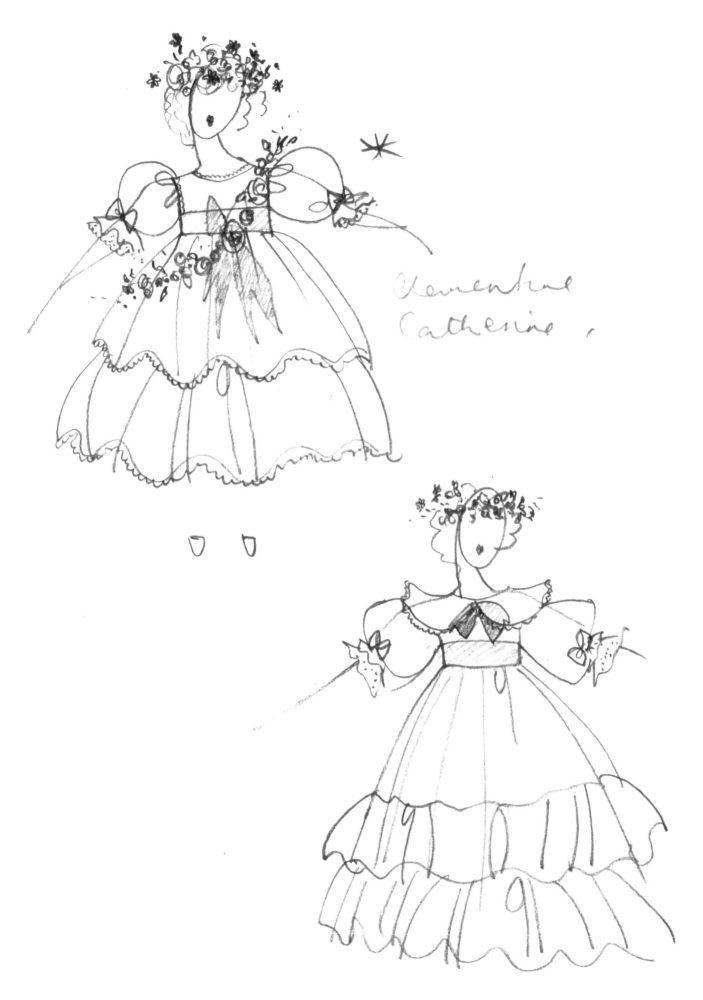

Clementine
Catherine

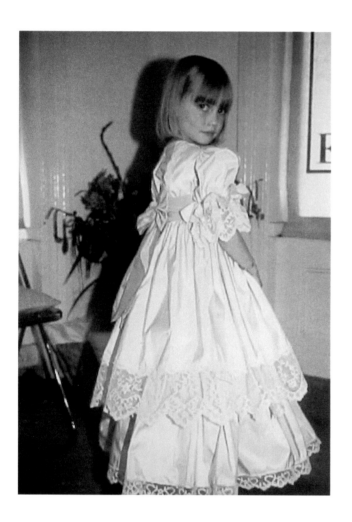

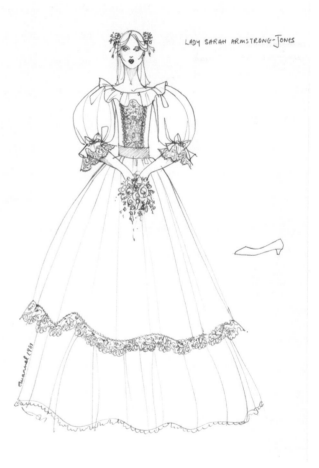

LADY SARAH ARMSTRONG-JONES

Opposite Some early sketches of designs for the dresses for Catherine and Clementine.

Above left Clementine, the youngest bridesmaid, trying on her final dress in the studio.

Above right This sketch of the dress worn by Lady Sarah Armstrong-Jones is from the official press release.

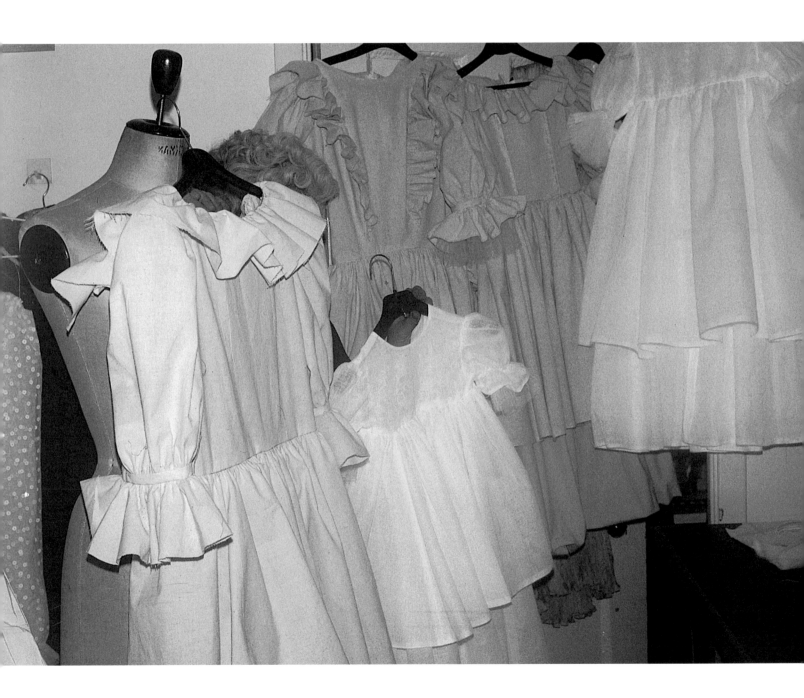

Organizing fittings for the bridesmaids was quite an undertaking because they lived in different parts of the country. Each bridesmaid needed several fittings and these could often be done individually, but particularly towards the end of the preparations, when we needed to schedule fittings and rehearsals with everyone together, we had to spend a lot of time on the telephone trying to co-ordinate everyone's diaries. It was important to make sure that the proportions were the same for each girl. Judging from the quantity of fabric from the bridesmaids dresses that we still have stored in our trunk of royal wedding leftovers – frills and frills of it – we must have made a lot of alterations to get them exactly right, neither too short nor too long.

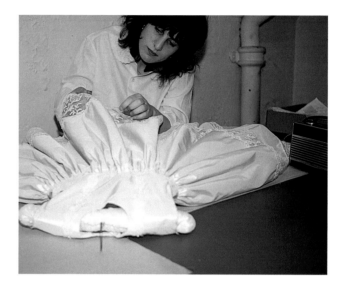

Nevertheless, when we did manage to get everyone together, the bridesmaids brought a lot of fun to the fittings. They were young and pretty and thought it was incredibly exciting that they were going to be part of this enormous wedding. They would rush in, fling their arms around Diana and kiss her, and we had quite a job getting them to stand still. On one particular day, they all arrived on roller-skates, which they insisted on wearing with their toiles during the fittings. It was total chaos.

The next time we saw the girls all together they were standing in St. Paul's behind the soon-to-be Princess of Wales. They clearly loved their dresses and with their flower circlets and their baskets of fresh flowers they looked quite angelic – what a transformation!

"And so there they were in their bridesmaids outfits, looking all official and 'don't I look smart'. And then you lower your eyes and they'd got roller-skates on. I wish we had a picture of that; that would have been great!"

Opposite The bridesmaids' toiles hanging up in the studio. These, like Diana's dress, had to be kept in the closely guarded safe overnight.
Above right Elizabeth puts the finishing touches to one of the bridesmaid's dresses, embroidering the lace at the hem of the skirt.

THE LACE

While we were still at college, Elizabeth loved hunting out bits and pieces of vintage fabric, lace and ribbon at flea markets, but when we started Emanuel we were creating so many intricate dresses and using so much antique lace on them that we had to visit auction houses to search out further supplies. This was a time when not many people were buying vintage textiles, so we were was able to pick up material quite easily. We would come home with bags and bags of the stuff, which we'd then empty out onto a table to discover what they contained. We never actually knew what was inside until we opened up the bags. We would then clean and sometimes dye or tint pieces before using them on our gowns.

We would often contact the Royal School of Needlework for help with whitening or repairing antique lace, and built up a rapport with Miss Bartlett, the Head of the Work Room. We had planned to use a wonderfully intricate piece of lace, found by Caroline's mother at auction, somewhere in Yorkshire. However, late in the day, we were contacted by Miss Bartlett, offering us two pieces of historic lace from their collection. How fitting to think that a piece of royal lace donated by Queen Mary herself would form the central bodice lace on Diana's dress, and once again become part of a royal gown. When we explained the significance of this lace to Diana she was genuinely touched.

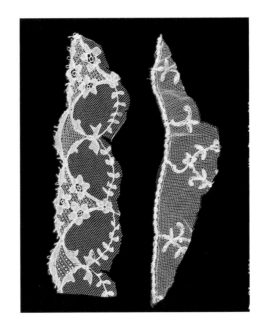

Above Unused samples of the Queen Mary lace that were kindly given to us by the Royal School of Needlework in London.

ROYAL SCHOOL OF NEEDLEWORK   25 Princes Gate, London SW7 1QE.   Tel. 01 589 0077

Ref WR/MB/MA

8th July 1981

Elizabeth and David Emanuel
26A Brook St
Mayfair
London W1

Dear Elizabeth and David

   I am sending the only information about the lace we have supplied
for you, as follows.-

1. Flounce of Carrick – ma – Cross lace, given to the Royal School of
Needlework by Her Majesty Queen Mary. (date of gift not known)

2. Small pieces of Carrick – ma – Cross and applied Honiton lace, also
Honiton edging. (if you have used them ?)

   These pieces of lace were given to the Royal School of Needlework
for a lace fund set up during World War II to make up as articles, such
as lace cushions, scent sachets, nightdress cases etc. These items were
sold and the proceeds were used for a fund for the Soldiers, Sailors and
Airmens Association.

   I do hope ~~hope~~ this information will be helpful to you.

   If you have any of the lace over (which I doubt), I would be grateful
if we could have those pieces back.

   Hoping all is well with you.

                              Yours sincerely

                              Margaret Bartlett

                              (Miss Margaret Bartlett BEM)
                              Head of Work Room

Roger Watson Laces
126 Derby Road
Nottingham   (0602) 43425

Roger Watson Laces is a very small
Company specializing in three de types
of Lace, all made on Schiffli
Embroidery Machines; Guipure Lace,
Macramé Lace, and Embroidered Net Lace.

Mr Roger Watson, whose Uncle and Grandfather
were also Lace Manufacturers, has been in
the Lace Trade all his life, and started
his separate business 12 years ago

Embroidered Net Lace is self-explanatory,
And consists of stitching yarn onto
a Net Background to create a design on
the Net.   In order to create the most
beautiful effect, it is best to use a
fine yarn to make the bulk of the
pattern and different effects, and then
to outline this with a thick Cord.
Strictly speaking, only this type of Lace
Should be called Needlerun Lace, and
because of its high price, none of this
Lace had been made in Nottingham
for approx. 20 years.

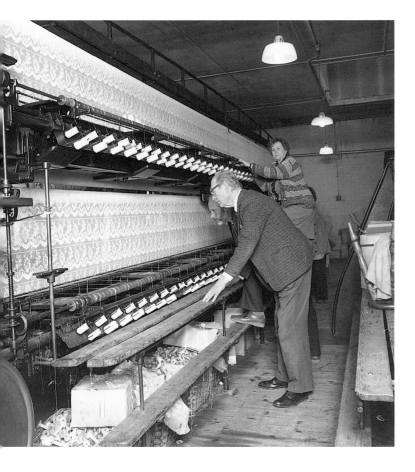

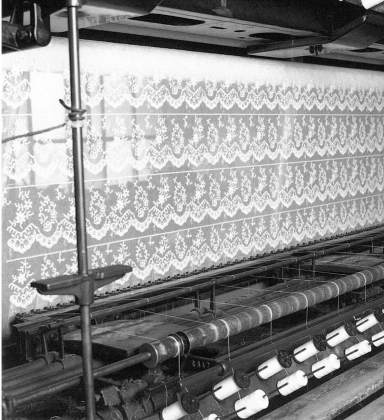

Opposite, above and overleaf In addition to our own antique lace already included in the flounces, we asked one of our regular suppliers, Roger Watson Laces, to design a range of matching lace that would form the trim on the remainder of Diana's dress and train, as well as being used extensively throughout the bridesmaids dresses. The design in the lace was interpreted from the Carrick-ma-Cross lace used in the flounce that we provided.

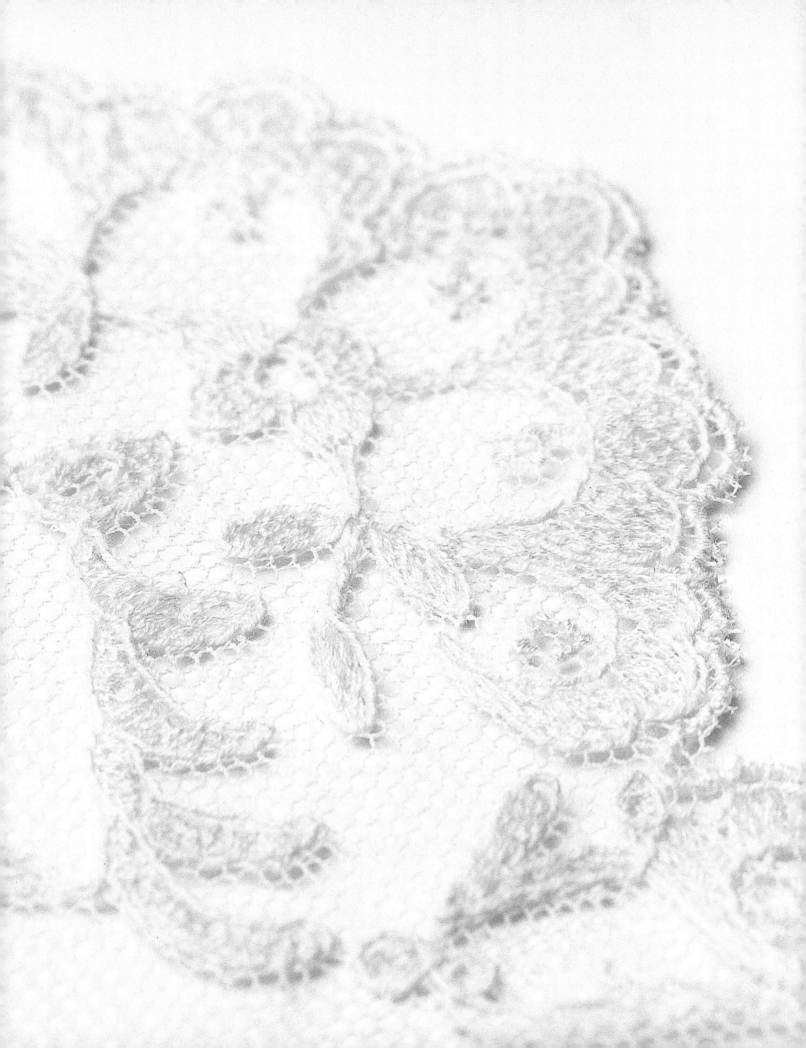

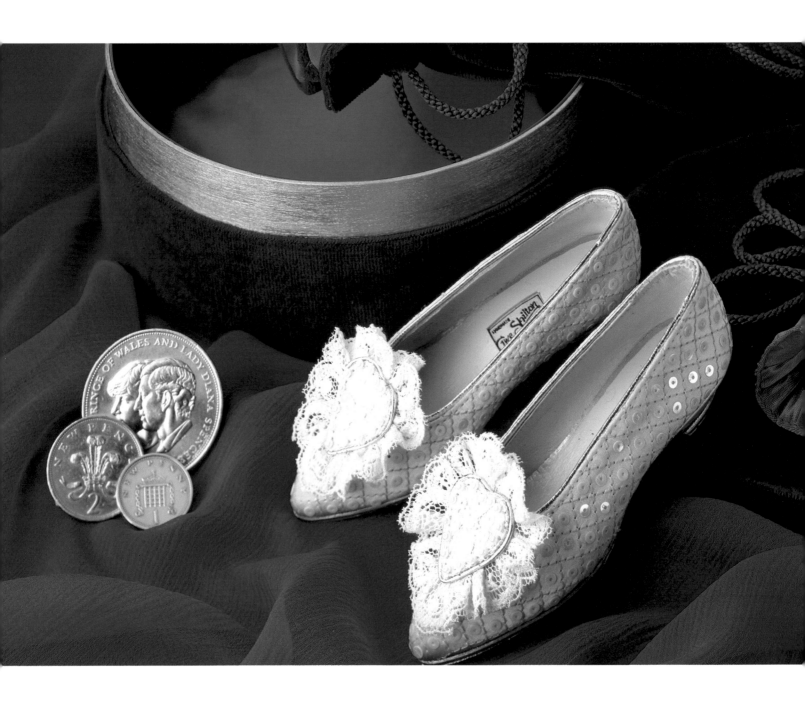

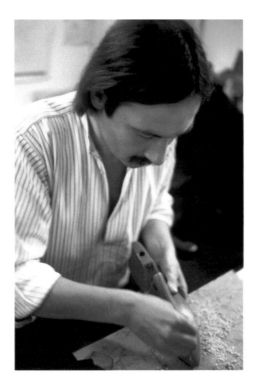
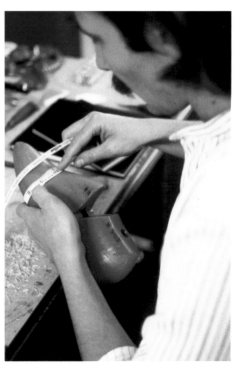

THE SHOES

At Emanuel, we had worked with several shoemakers to create designs for our fashion shows, and occasionally one of our clients would want shoes specially made. We particularly liked Clive Shilton's shoes, which were all completely handmade. We deliberately chose him rather than one of the larger shoe houses to design and make the wedding shoes for Diana because, aside from the quality of his craftsmanship, Clive is a discreet, very quiet man, and we felt that we could trust him. We wanted to keep the project very personal and very special.

Opposite Clive Shilton made a miniature pair of the wedding shoes as a gift for Diana. The coins next to them reveal their tiny size.
Above Clive working on the lasts for Diana's shoes.

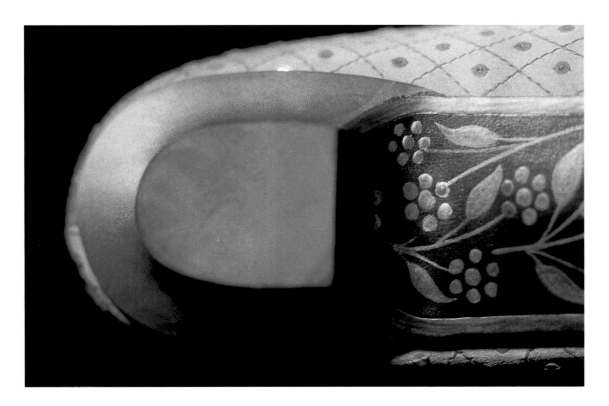

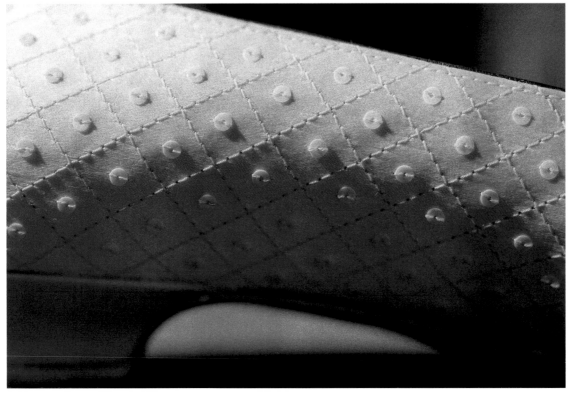

Accustomed as we were to keeping everything a secret, we didn't disclose anything about the design of the dress, even to Clive. Fortunately, he was aware of the style of clothes for which we were best known and was able to make a guess that the wedding gown would be very romantic and detailed.

We sent him a piece of the taffeta that the dress was made from, hoping that he might be able to use the same fabric for the shoes, but unfortunately it was too fine. In the end, he used silk duchess satin, which is a much heavier. This was also woven by Stephen Walters, who dyed it to match precisely the colour of the silk taffeta that we were using for the dress. Clive was also given a small amount of lace, as well as sequins and pearls to use on the shoes. In fact, there were 542 mother-of-pearl sequins on each pair, each one knotted by hand.

After measuring Diana's feet, the first thing Clive worked on was the creation of the last, one of the most important tasks in making any pair of shoes. He wanted to create a very elegant shape, and he did this with a tiny fluted heel made out of bits of leather and wood. A completely flat shoe would not have looked right, but the heels needed to be very low because Diana was so tall.

The design of the shoes evolved from that shape. They had a straight top-line cut, which Clive was making very fashionable at the time. He devised various alternative trims to go on the front. He showed all these to Diana, who immediately chose a heart-shaped trim. Another heart was engraved on the sole of the shoe along with a "C" and a "D".

Opposite Clive Shilton was known for the exquisite detailing and perfect finishes of his shoes. The royal wedding slippers were fantastically intricate – there were 542 mother-of-pearl sequins on each pair – and even the soles were hand-painted, with the letters "C" and "D" entwined with a heart. Two left and two right shoes were actually made, and the choice of which to use was made after the final fitting.

"WE FELT VERY DEEPLY HONOURED TO BE ASKED TO DESIGN THE SHOES, WHICH SOUNDS TERRIBLY OLD-FASHIONED NOW, BUT IT WAS A REALLY, REALLY SPECIAL THING TO BE WORKING ON ... THIS WAS A STATE OCCASION AND WE WANTED TO DEMONSTRATE THE BEST OF BRITISH CRAFTSMANSHIP, AND I THINK THAT WE CAME UP WITH SOMETHING TRULY EXQUISITE."

Clive Shilton, Shoe designer

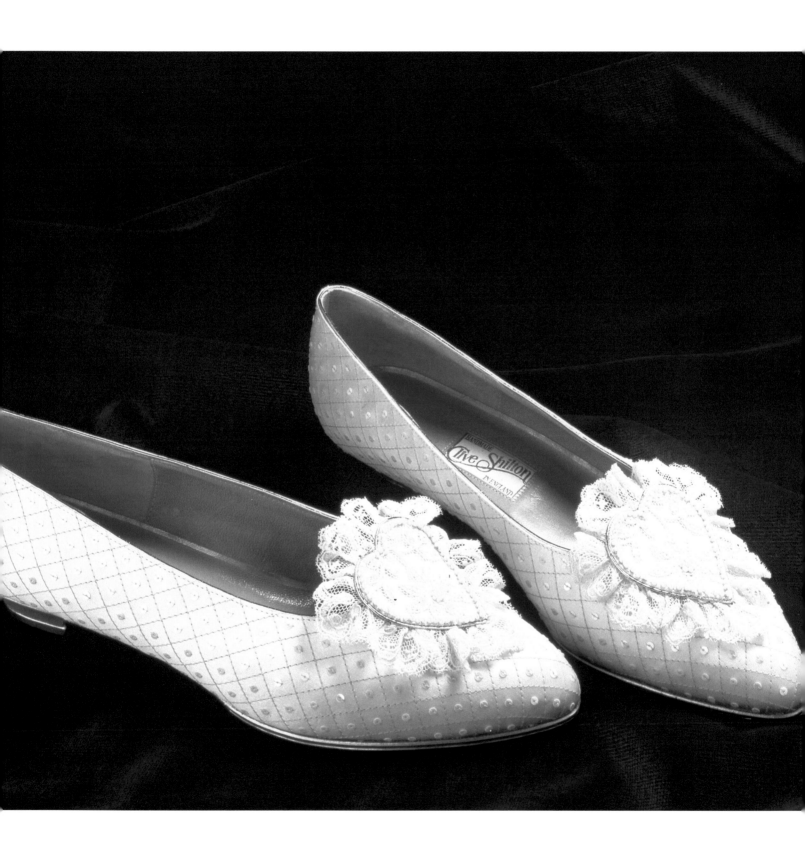

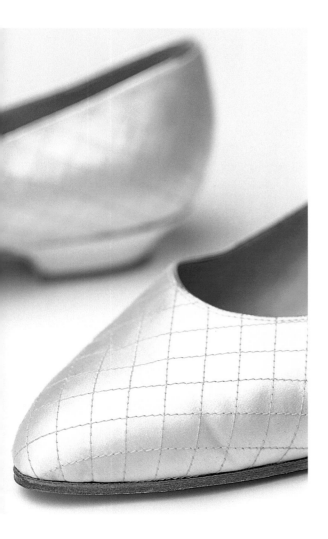

Throughout the process of the dress fittings, Clive also had to keep adjusting the shoes. He saw her several times, always at Brook Street, which was easier for Diana with her busy schedule. Whereas we could alter things, Clive had to start again. Although you can stretch a pair of shoes by adding and restretching, you can't take away. Alterations are very limited with shoes.

For the wedding rehearsal, we wanted to try to allow Diana to feel exactly what it was going to be like to wear the dress on the day. So we gave her a big petticoat and Clive made a mock-up pair of shoes. As she walked up the aisle in St. Paul's, she would be able to tell whether there were going to be any problems with the shoes, whether they were uncomfortable in any way or too flat.

In the past, when apprentice shoemakers reached the end of their apprenticeship, which took many years, they had to make a miniature shoe to demonstrate their skills. (Making a small shoe is much more difficult than making a full-size; for a start, the component parts are tiny.) Clive came up with the wonderful idea of making a miniature pair of the wedding shoes, which he presented to Diana in a beautiful blue velvet box.

Above left These practice shoes were worn with the petticoat for the rehearsal at St. Paul's to give Diana an idea of how they would feel. They were also used to check the length of the dress.
Opposite A close-up of the heart design on the front of the shoes, which were made with some of the same lace as used on the dress. They weren't made of glass, but they were real Cinderella slippers.

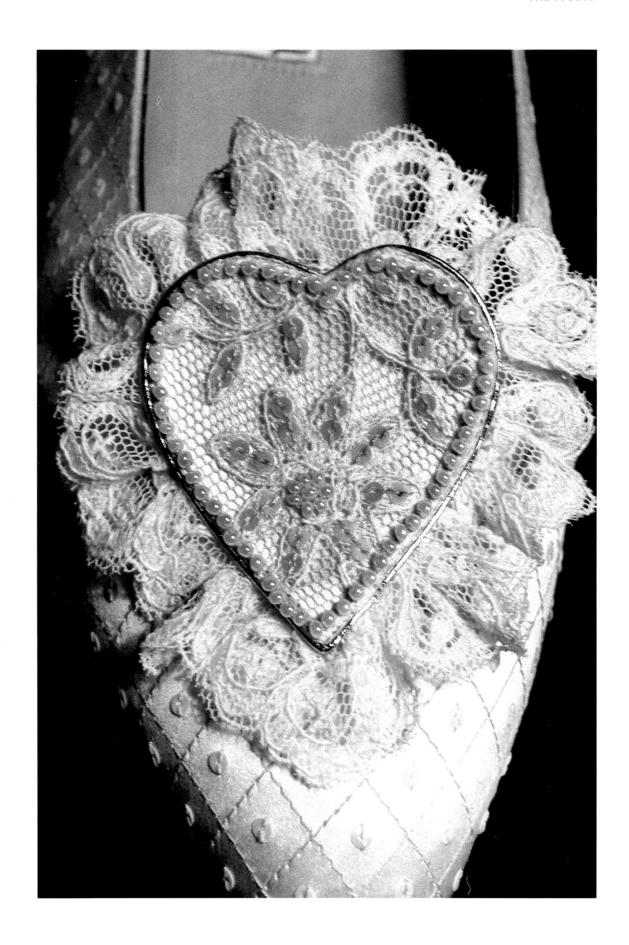

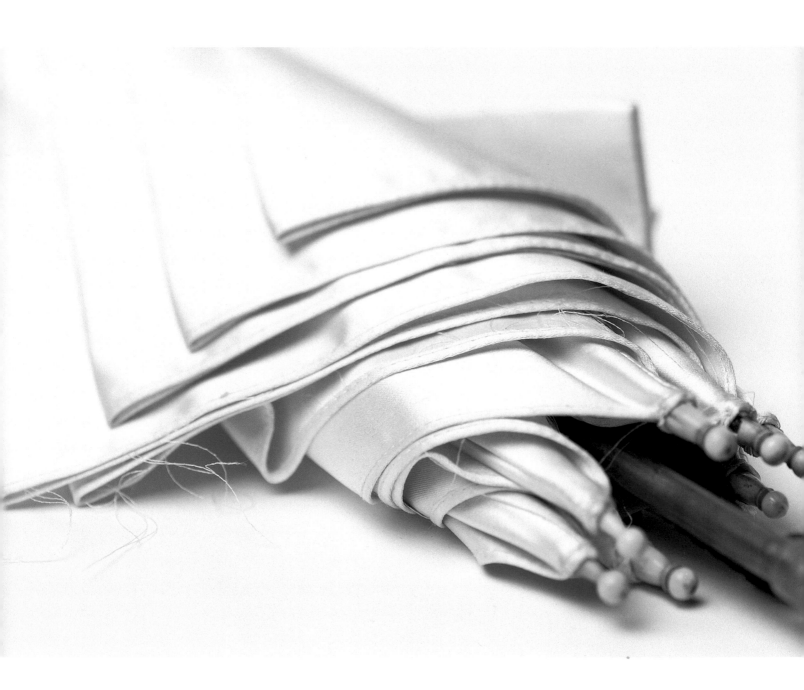

Above We decided to make Diana a parasol so that in the event of rain she would stay dry and still look pretty. The original, vintage parasol came from Phillips at auction and was covered in the same ivory silk as the dress. It was then waterproofed.

Opposite, left This sketch of the parasol and a little pochette were included in the press embargo.

Opposite, right The silk parasol was trimmed with the same lace as used on the dress, and also hand-embroidered with tiny pearls and sequins.

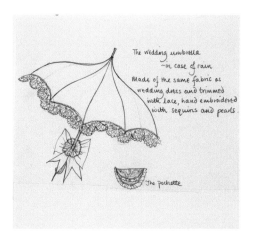

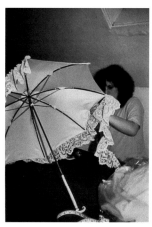

THE LOOK

As fashion designers, we were responsible for creating not only the wedding gown, but the whole look. It was not just a frock but a whole stage production. We knew that there is nothing worse than seeing somebody stepping out of a limousine – or, in this case, a glass carriage – and thinking, "That dress looks fabulous, but...".

When we were sketching our first ideas, the dress was our main focus, but we were still very aware that shoes, hair, make-up, flowers, all these things are equally important if the bride is to look truly wonderful.

So we liaised not only with the shoemaker but also with the florists – both Longmans, who were responsible for Diana's bouquet, and Edward Goodyear, who did the little flower baskets and circlets for the bridesmaids. We suggested that Barbara Daly (who we had worked with on numerous photo shoots and was famous for her amazing film work) would be the perfect person to do her makeup, while Diana brought her own hairdresser, Kevin Shanley, who had been styling her hair for years.

THE FLOWERS

We knew that we wanted Diana to have a large bouquet. The scale of the dress meant that a small one would have simply disappeared. In fact, the massive bouquet that Longman's created for her set a new vogue for wedding bouquets, which had until then been relatively small.

We had to give Longmans an idea of the scale of the dress was like but without giving them any details, and although we were getting plenty of practice at this, it was still quite tricky. In the end, we gave them a little sketch to show the rough shape and we also let them know the colour.

David Longman met with Diana twice, the first time to discuss the bouquet generally and the second time to submit sketches and a mock-up made with silk flowers. Diana approved all their suggestions. A special request from the Palace was that the bouquet should include some mimosa yellow roses called "Mountbatten", developed by the Harkness brothers in memory of Lord Louis Mountbatten.

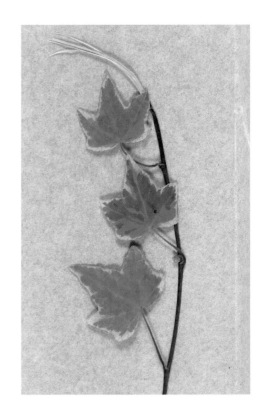

Above right These miniature ivy leaves were used in Diana's bouquet, along with tradescantia leaves, to provide trailing foliage.
Opposite The sketch, drawn by Doris Wellham the Head Florist at Longmans, of the design.
Overleaf The embargoed press release from Longmans provides details of all the flowers they used in the bouquet.

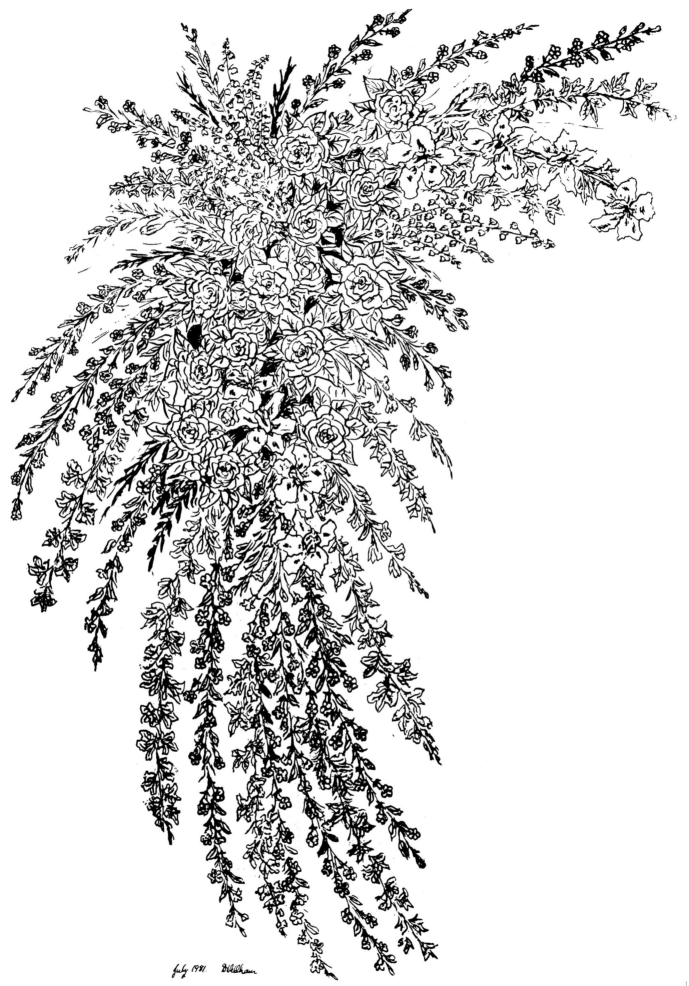

July 1981. DWilliam

131

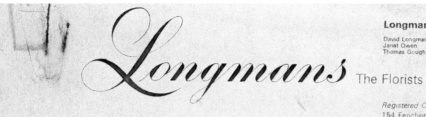

Longmans Limited

David Longman
Janet Owen
Thomas Gough

Please reply to

Registered Office:
154 Fenchurch Street EC3M 7LD
Telephone: 01.623 8414
Telex No.: 883497

7 Ludgate Circus EC4M 7LD
Telephone: 01.353 0146

22 The Market
Covent Garden WC2
Telephone: 01.836 6059

7 Gees Court
Oxford Street W1
Telephone: 01.935 3352

The Plant House
202 Long Lane SE1
Telephone: 01.403 1713

at Army & Navy
Victoria Street SW1
Telephone: 01.828 4721

WEDDING BOUQUET CARRIED BY LADY DIANA SPENCER
FOR HER MARRIAGE TO H.R.H. THE PRINCE OF WALES

Restricted information until 29th July 1981
0900 hours

The Bouquet is the gift of the Worshipful Company of Gardeners
of London. It is presented in accordance with long established
privilege and rights of the Company to present bouquets of
flowers to the Royal family on State occasions and for weddings.

The company appointed Longmans Ltd., an old established firm of
City florists to prepare the bouquet. Mr. David M.H. Longman,
the Managing Director and a Past Master of the Company was
responsible for the designs and preparation of the Bouquet.
His father, the late M.H. Longman had a similar responsibility in
preparing the wedding for Her Majesty the Queen in 1947, then
H.R.H. Princess Elizabeth.

Mr. Longman had sketches of bouquets prepared, and made samples
in polyester silk flowers. These were discussed with Lady Diana
and the dressmakers were consulted as well. From these
discussions a final sample was made, submitted to and approved by
the Bride.

The Bouquet is of a shower design but considerably larger than
modern trends being some 42" long and 15" wide. It is essentially
a flowing bouquet with a natural graceful look, reminiscent of
Edwardian days without the heavy greenery of that era. It is
well balanced, and although heavier than most carried nowadays
the distribution should not be too tiresome for the Bride.

The centre of the Bouquet is comprised of a cluster of gardenia
flowers supported by golden Earl Mountbatten roses (see separate
note appended) from the centre flows a graceful cascade of white
Odontoglossum orchids which have a soft golden eye. The main
strength of the shower is of pips of Stephanotis, falling in
three main drops, each drop supported by miniature ivy and
tradescantia leaves.

Registered in England No. 174659

Longmans Limited

David Longman
Janet Owen
Thomas Gough

Longmans The Florists

Registered Office:
154 Fenchurch Street EC3M 7LD
Telephone: 01 623 8414
Telex No.: 883497

7 Ludgate Circus EC4M 7LD
Telephone: 01 353 0146

22 The Market
Covent Garden WC2
Telephone: 01 836 6059

7 Gees Court
Oxford Street W1
Telephone: 01 935 3352

The Plant House
202 Long Lane SE1
Telephone: 01 403 1713

at Army & Navy
Victoria Street SW1
Telephone: 01 828 4721

lease reply to

A spray of orchids rise from the centre and is surrounded by lily-of-the-valley and white freesia.

The bouquet is predominately white, through cream of the gardenias to the gold of the roses. The backing is green slightly wild in nature, with myrtle from Osborne House and veronica from the Bishop of Norwich, both grown from bushes struck from cuttings taken from Queen Victoria's Bouquet.

The Bouquet was beautifully scented, as the majority of flowers used are heavily perfumed. There perfumes should blend together to give that lovely fragrance of an English summer garden.

The flowers and foliage are all British grown.

GARDENIAS	-	From	Kent
STEPHANOTIS	-	"	Guernsey
FREESIA	-	"	"
ODONTOGLOSSUM ORCHID	- ROYAL WEDDING	"	Sussex
LILY OF THE VALLEY	-	"	Surrey
EARL MOUNTBATTEN ROSES	-	"	Hertfordshire
HEDERA (IVY)	-	"	Kent
TRADESCANTIA	-	"	London
MYRTLE	-	"	Isle of Wight
VERONICA (HEBE)	-	"	Norwich

Registered in England No. 174659

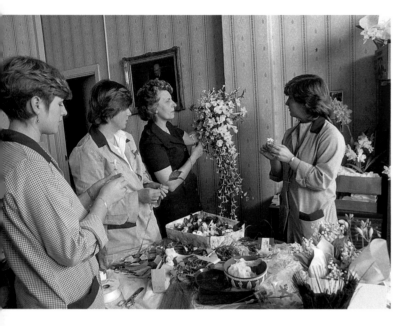

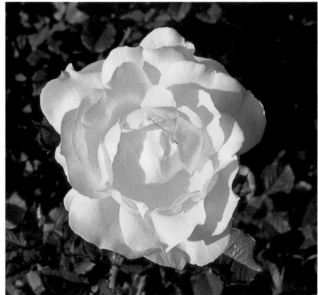

The flowers for Diana's bouquet came from all over England. It was quite a nightmare for Longmans to get all the flowers together and at the same time maintain the tight security demanded on the content and the design. The two most difficult flowers were the white odontoglossum orchids and the gardenias. The former were grown by a nursery in Sussex and were supplied on the plant so that they would be really fresh and in good condition. The gardenias were no longer grown in Britain as a cut flower, only as plants with blooms on them, but David Longman managed to collect some twenty or so plants and had a nursery in Kent grow them on for him.

Three bouquets were made in all. The first was used for the practice the evening before the wedding and was subsequently displayed in Longmans' shop window. The second was made in the early hours of the wedding morning and delivered to St James Palace. The third was taken to Buckingham Palace at about 10.00AM, to be used for the formal photographs. These bouquets were accompanied to their destinations by a police motorcycle escort through the closed roads.

Above left Longman's begin to assemble Diana's wedding bouquet.
Above right The Mountbatten rose, which was incorporated into the bouquet as a special request of the palace. Its gorgeous yellow colour inspired our bridesmaids dresses.
Opposite Longman's final bouquet interpreted our vision perfectly. We were thrilled that it complemented the scale and grandeur of the dress and the occasion.

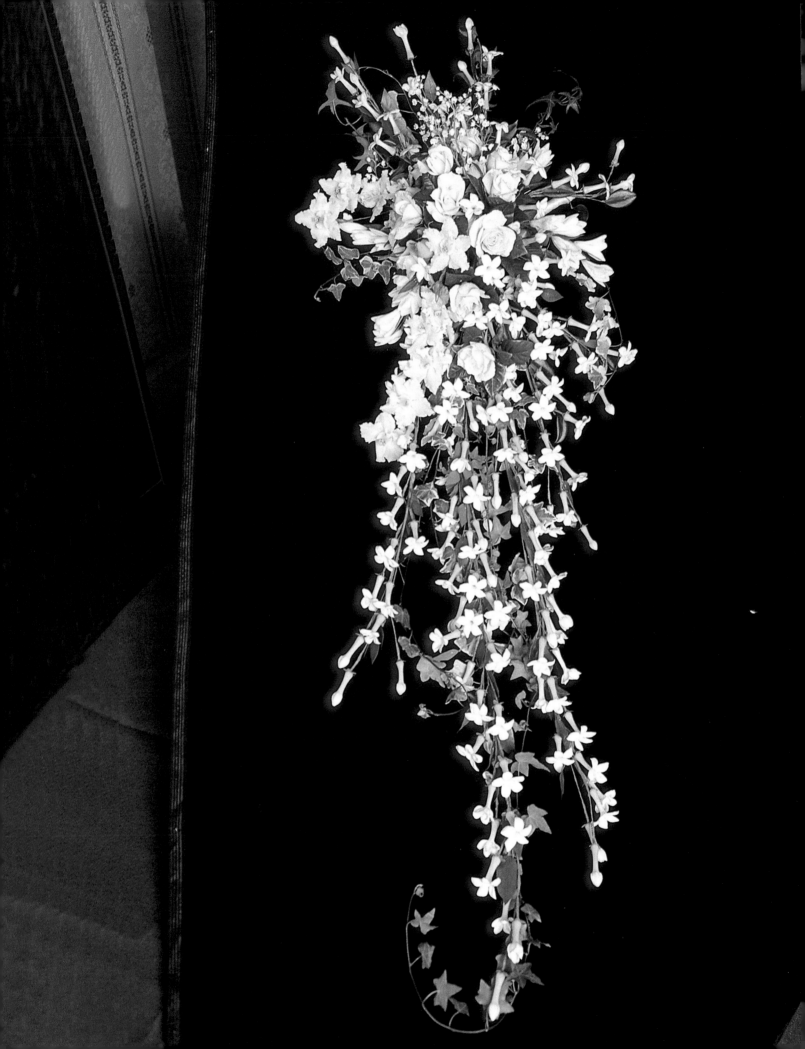

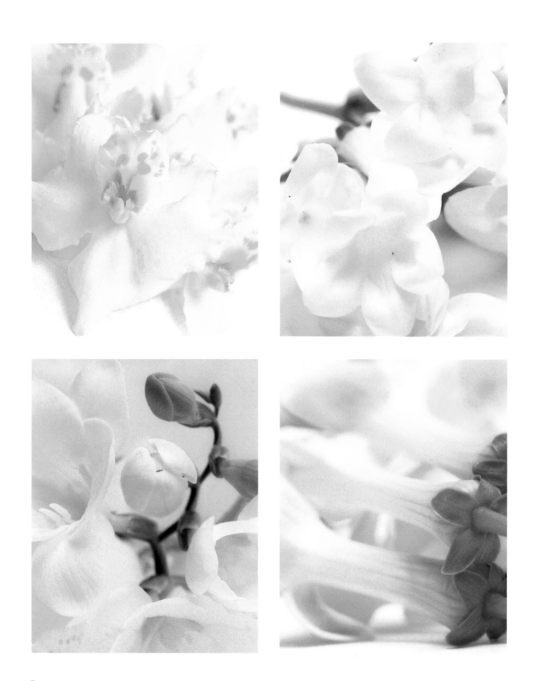

Top left Odontoglossum "Royal Wedding"
Top Right Stephanotis Floribunda **Bottom left** Fresia
Bottom right Stephanotis Floribunda

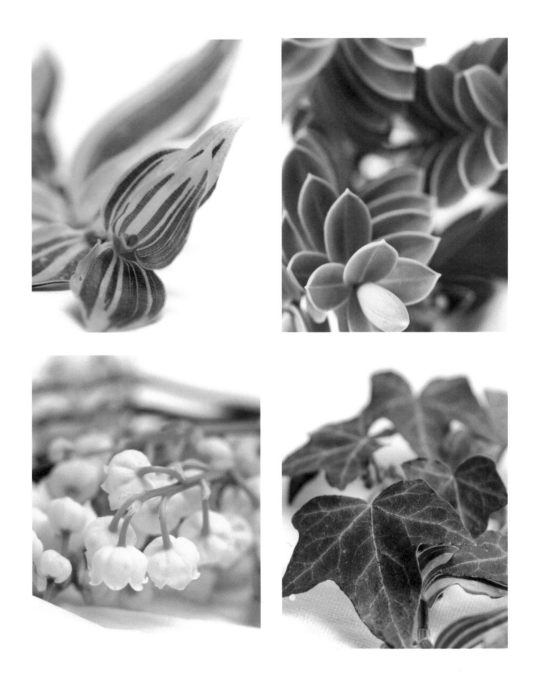

Top left Tradescanthia **Top Right** Veronica,
Bottom left Lily of the Valley **Bottom right** Hedera

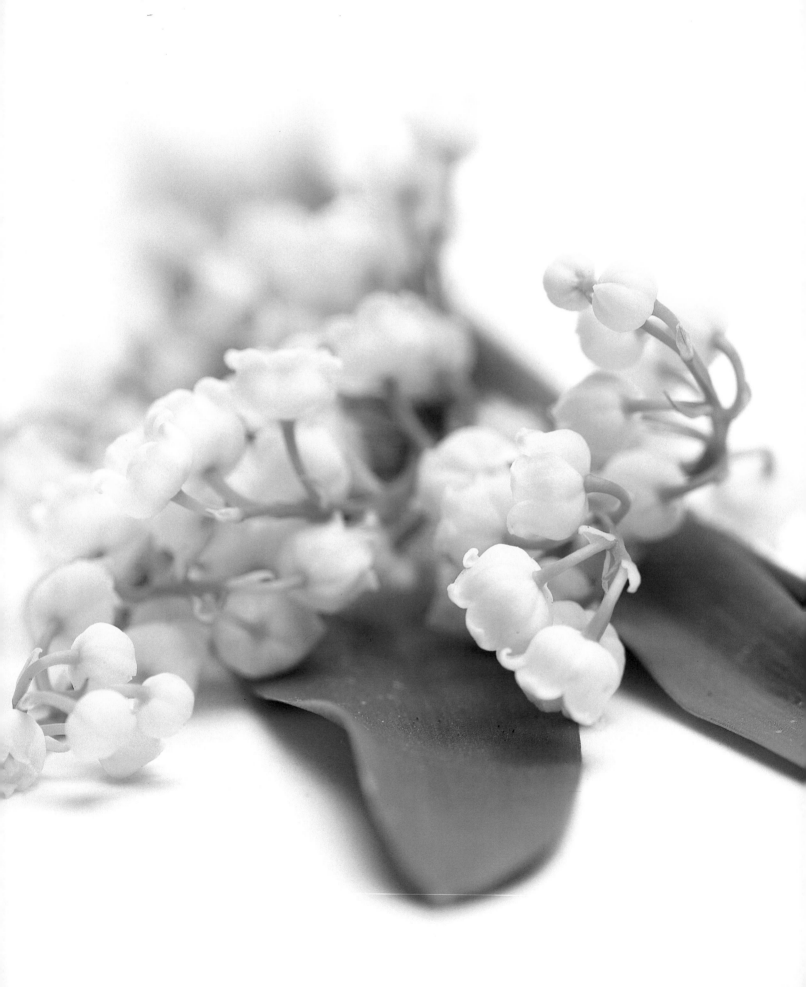

"A happy, confident and relaxed Diana leaving Brook Street after her final fitting, by now accustomed to the mayhem and madness of the waiting paparazzi, who had been joined by television news crews from around the globe. By this time, even we had grown used to the constant press presence, and every entrance and exit was planned like a military operation. Unseen in this photograph, our PA Caroline became doorman to add to her many other responsibilities."

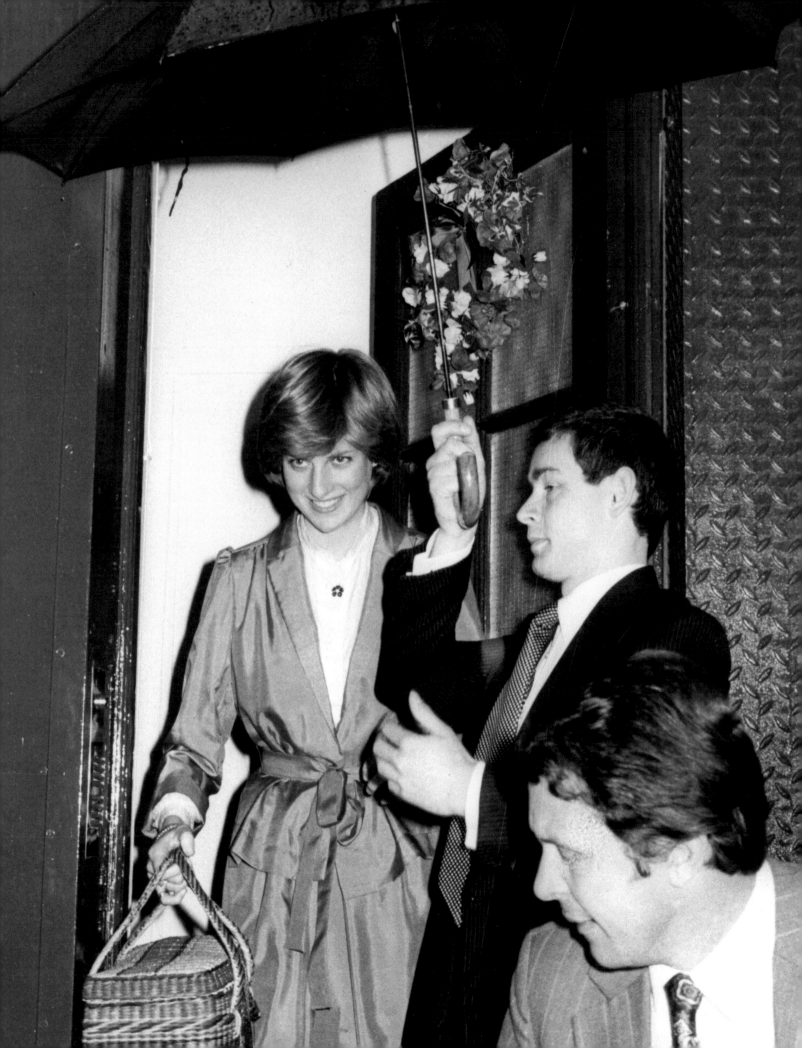

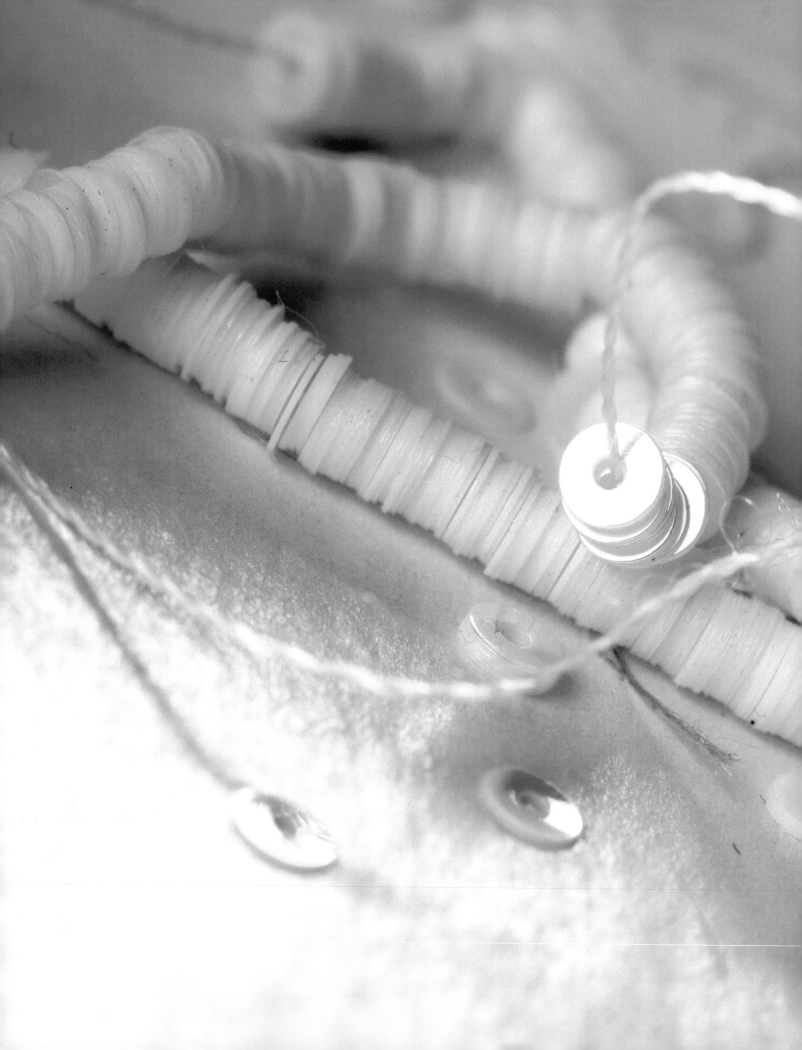

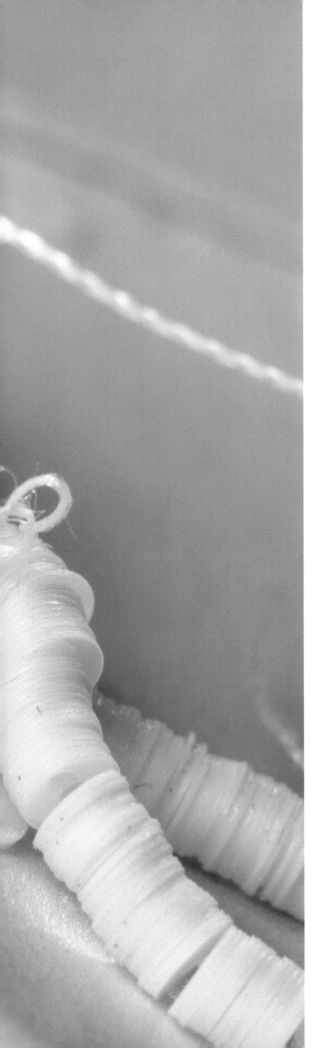

"Over the years, a lot of people have come up to us, across the world, who've queued up for hours and hours to see the gown in some sort of display, and they say they had no idea of the amount of detail in it. We're talking about hours and hours of work – a pure labour of love."

THE EMBROIDERY

It was decided that Elizabeth would start embroidering all the twinkly bits – everything that glistened – on the dress. But when you start on this kind of project, you really don't appreciate how long it's going to take. We had hundreds of metres of lace that all had to be embroidered with pearls and tiny mother-of-pearl sequins – all of which had to follow the intricate design of the lace, because we wanted the dress to be magical, to twinkle like something out of a fairy story.

But at a certain stage we began to panic because it truly seemed as though it would take forever. The trouble was that all our team were already more than fully occupied and we didn't want to involve any new staff at this stage. Eventually we brought in Elizabeth's mother, who was was very nimble with a needle – she loved making petit-point cushions – and we also persuaded Caroline's mother to come and work for us. We warned them that they would be working from nine in the morning until eight o'clock at night, but in fact it felt like a real family thing with all of us sewing this dress together.

We decided we would have to send the veil out to be embroidered. Who better to call upon than our trusted friend and embroiderer, "Miss Peggy" Umpelby at S. Lock Ltd. We asked her to hand-embroider a staggering 10,000 3mm sequins onto the veil. She decided that because of the secrecy of the whole project, she would do all this at home. She spent the best part of two weeks with a huge tambour frame in her living room – large enough to take the veil, which measured 11½ foot by 40 foot. The only thing that annoyed Miss Peggy was her friends at work asking why, after two weeks holiday (as she had told them), she did not have a better sun tan.

"It was designed really just to catch the light, not so that you would actually see the sequins in the veil, but so that it would twinkle and look magical under the lights."

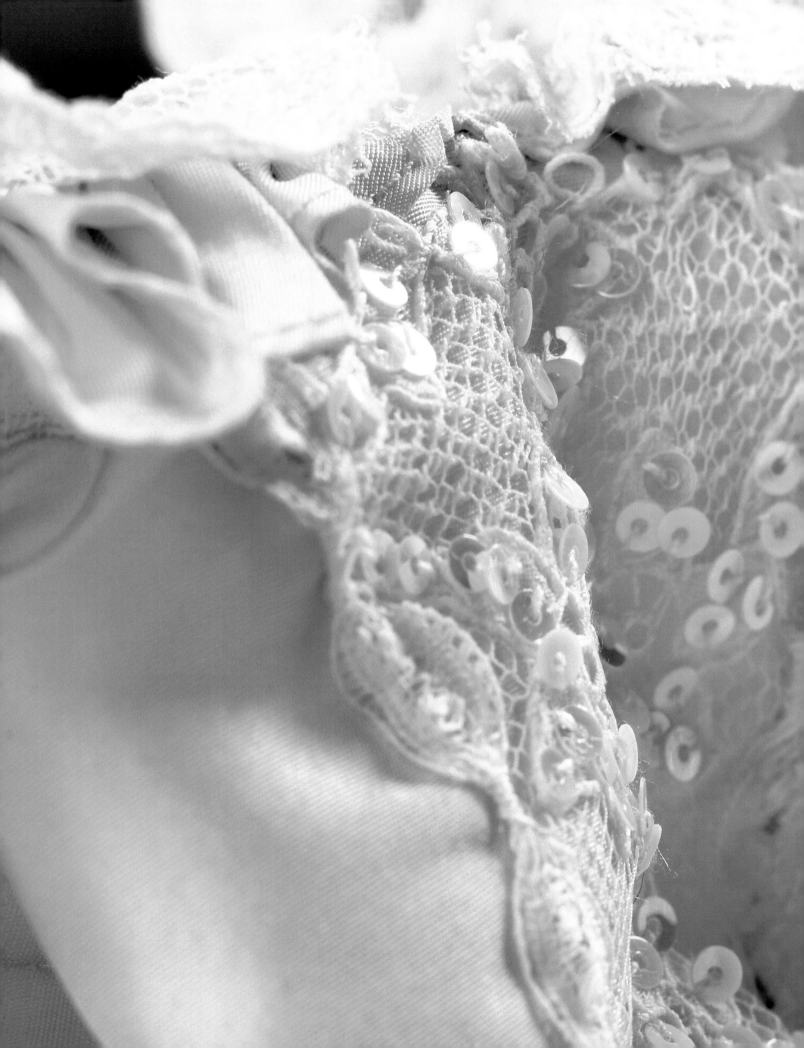

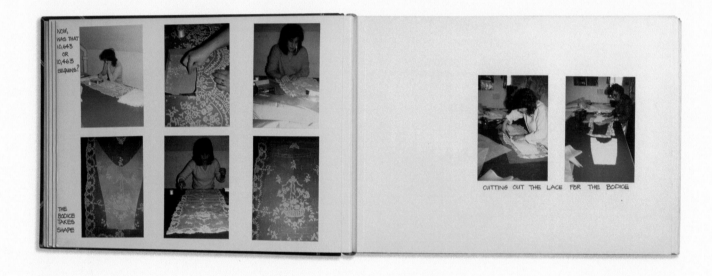

Above These pages from the album show the beautiful piece of
Queen Mary lace that was used on the front panel of the bodice
of the dress, and Elizabeth and Nina (far right) cutting it out and
attaching it to the silk taffeta panel.

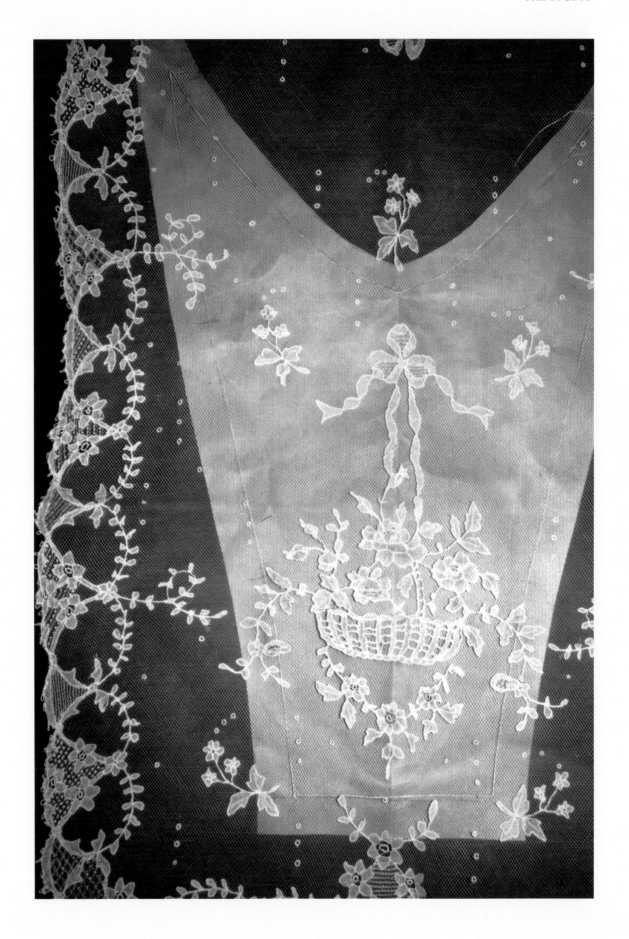

THE TRAIN

In all our thoughts about the design of the dress, we had to consider not only who was going to wear it and the importance of the occasion, but also where it would be worn. St. Paul's Catherdral is huge: the steps are monumental, the aisle is incredibly long, everything about it is enormous. And we wanted Diana to look like no princess had ever looked before. So we set out to discover the length of the longest royal wedding dress train. Eventually we discovered that one royal bride had had a twenty-three-foot train. We joked with Diana that we could go one better – in fact two feet better – and create a twenty-five-foot train. She loved the idea and laughed.

The biggest problem we faced was finding a space large enough for the fitting. We were still in our little studio in Brook Street, and there was no way there was enough room there. So David said to Diana, "Well, we'd better come to your place then, you've got more room in Buckingham Palace." She drove us there herself, just the three of us, and as we pulled up at the traffic lights, somebody looked across and did a quick double take at our royal chauffeur.

We were going to need a vast space so that we could lay out the whole train and give Diana the opportunity to sense the scale of the completed gown. We were given Princess Anne's bedroom as a make-shift fitting room and began the task at hand. However, there were lots of people – footmen and other palace staff – milling about. We explained to Diana that they would have to go – we had promised to keep everything about the dress a secret, after all – but she wasn't the royal princess yet and blushed at the prospect of giving out orders. In the end, David took charge and asked everybody to leave. (They probably weren't too impressed that

"My favourite picture of all is of Diana and she's at the top of the steps and the wind has caught her veil and the train and it's swept them to one side. It's just the most incredible picture — it's so dramatic and theatrical."

we were commandeering an entire floor!) We locked the doors at either end of the corridor and began work on the train in private.

The train, once it was laid out, took up the whole length of the corridor and seeing it there, even though this was only a calico mock-up, we could begin to imagine how it would look in all its glory spread out along the aisle of St. Paul's Cathedral. We decided that it looked a bit wide, so we trimmed it until we got the right shape. Then Diana practised walking up and down in it to see how it felt. Of course, it was very heavy because it was made of calico, but we assured her that the finished train, which would be of silk taffeta, would be much lighter. On the day, it did literally float over the carpet in St. Paul's.

Having cut the calico train into what looked like the perfect shape, we suddenly had an awful thought: we knew that the aisle at St. Paul's was very long, but what if it wasn't wide enough? So we made a discreet phone call to the cathedral, requesting a private visit. As soon as we got out of the taxi at St. Paul's we were recognized — our pictures had been in the press quite a lot by that stage — but once inside we were able to get our tapemeasures out and reassure ourselves that the train wasn't going to hit the legs of guests as Diana walked up the aisle.

We did several several trips to Buckingham Palace and had a scary experience after one of them. We were working until quite late and, unbeknown to us, everything closes down there at about 5.30PM. Suddenly, we found ourselves lost downstairs somewhere and couldn't find our way out. We were roaming around and getting worried that we might have to spend the night there. It was completely deserted and we were locked in!

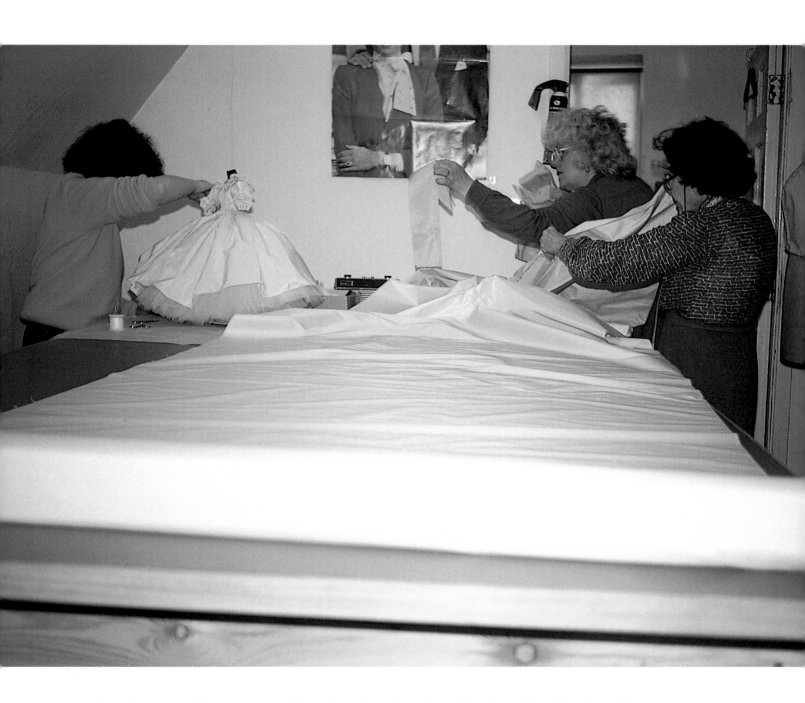

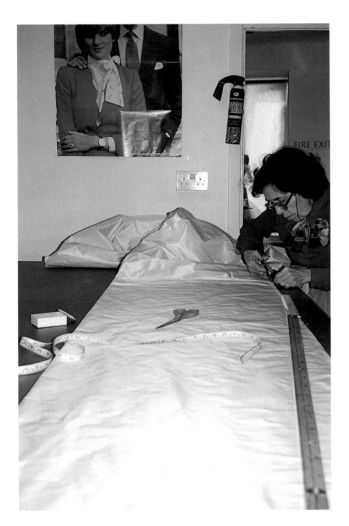

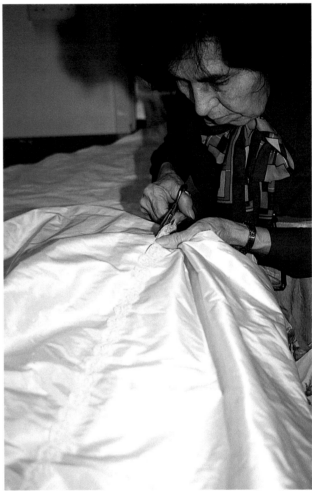

Opposite and above We had a whole corridor at Buckingham Palace in which to actually fit the twenty-five-foot train, but back at Brook Street poor Nina had much less space in which to cut and sew it – they were cramped into our tiny attic workroom.

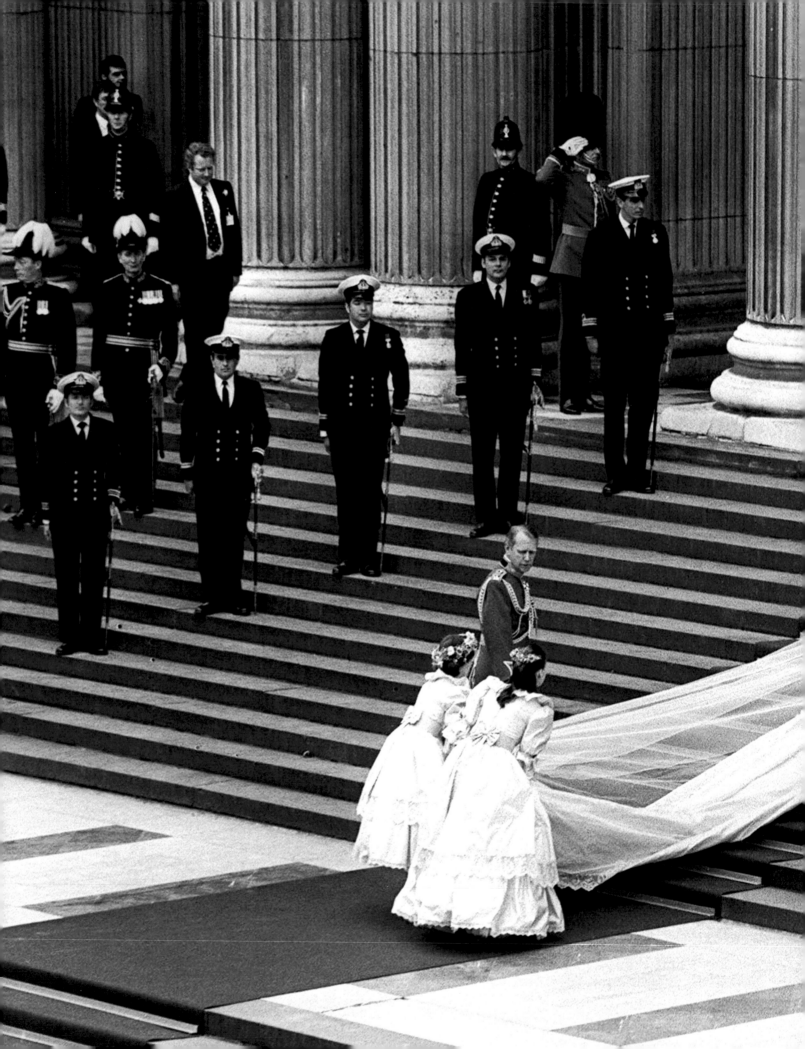

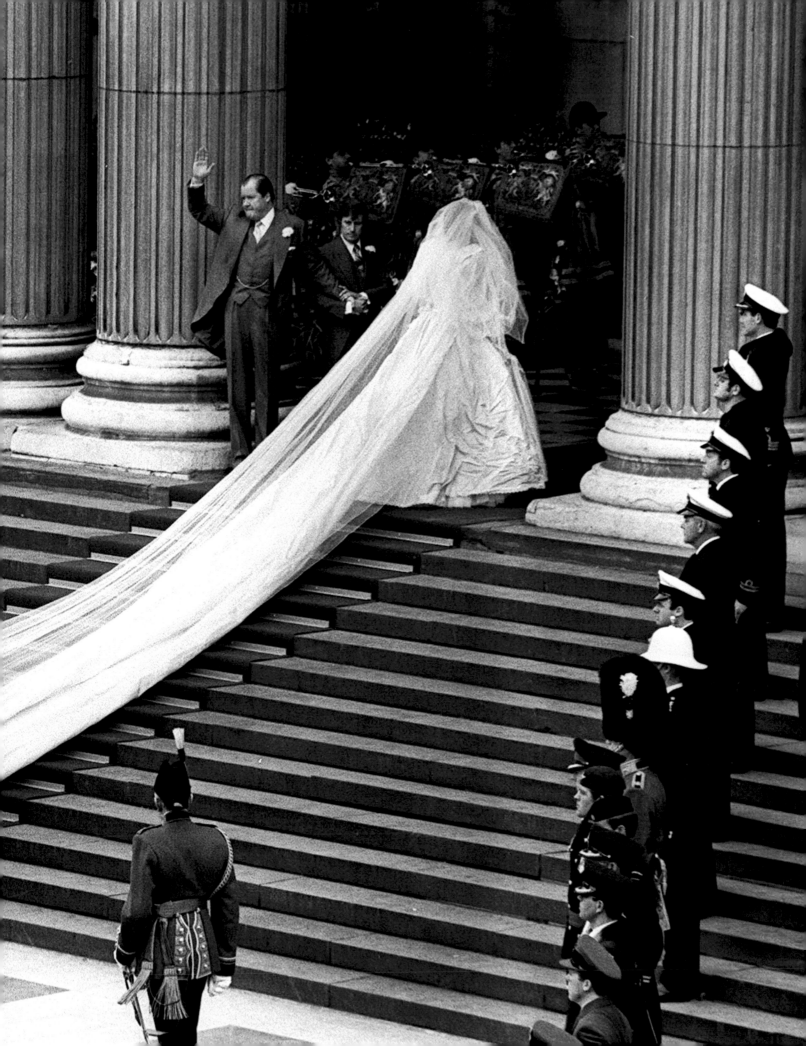

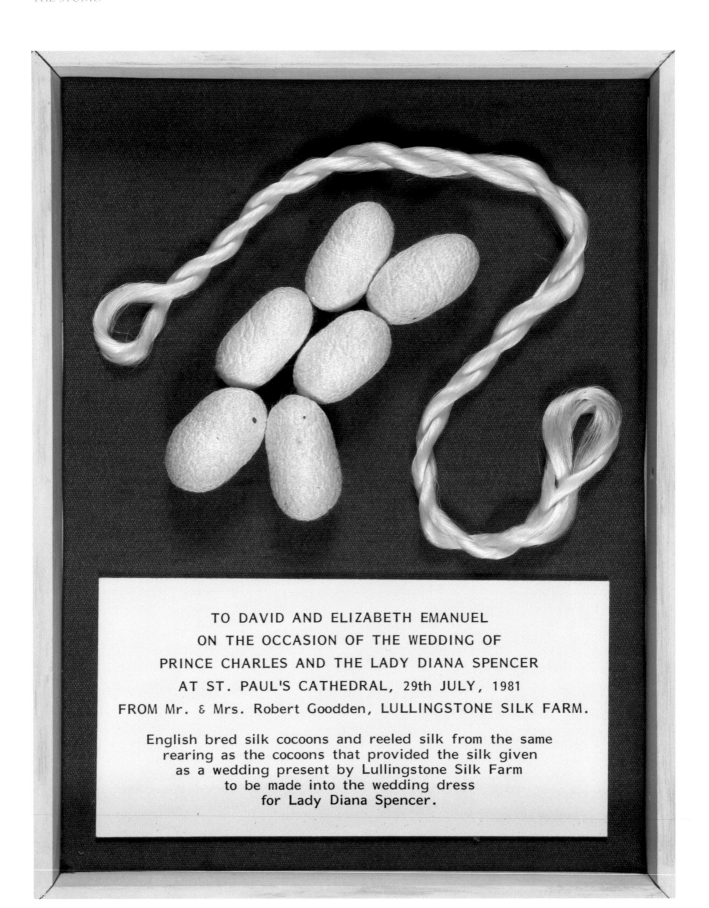

TO DAVID AND ELIZABETH EMANUEL
ON THE OCCASION OF THE WEDDING OF
PRINCE CHARLES AND THE LADY DIANA SPENCER
AT ST. PAUL'S CATHEDRAL, 29th JULY, 1981
FROM Mr. & Mrs. Robert Goodden, LULLINGSTONE SILK FARM.

English bred silk cocoons and reeled silk from the same
rearing as the cocoons that provided the silk given
as a wedding present by Lullingstone Silk Farm
to be made into the wedding dress
for Lady Diana Spencer.

"SOMETHING OLD, SOMETHING NEW..."

In keeping with tradition, we wanted to make sure that the bride had "Something old, something new, something borrowed, something blue". The old was represented by the piece of Queen Mary lace that we used on the bodice and flounces while the new was obviously the silk dress itself. The tiara that Diana wore was a Spencer family heirloom – so something borrowed – and to complete the tradition, we hand-sewed a little blue bow into the back of the dress.

In accordance with another wedding tradition, we commissioned a wonderful jeweller, Douglas Buchanan, to design and make a tiny, gold horseshoe from eighteen-carat Welsh gold, which we sewed into the back of the label of the dress. Nobody could see our private gift when the dress was being worn; it was just there as a little token, a little good luck charm, from us to Diana.

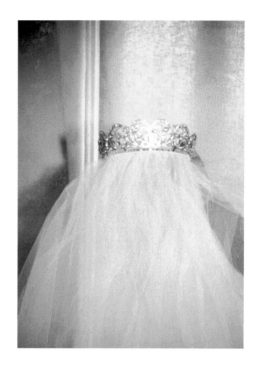

Opposite Lullingstone Silk Farm presented these silk cocoons and reeled silk to us in commemoration of the royal wedding. We had tried to keep the project as British as possible and whatever silk we could get from Lullingstone Silk Farm was used in the veil.

Above right A close-up of the face veil attached to the tiara, a Spencer family heirloom. The veil was hand-embroidered with thousands of mother-of-pearl sequins, each individually knotted and sewn into position.

155

THE FINISHED DRESS

The final security problem we had to solve was how to move the dress of the century from Brook Street to Clarence House on the day before the wedding. It was arranged that our PA Caroline's brother, Gerald, hire a van in his own name and drive it himself. We didn't want anybody to see anything as it came out of our building and we most definitely didn't want a van or anything else with the Emanuel name on it or, we feared, it would surely be hijacked. Although perhaps this was paranoia.

Each dress was meticulously packed and tissued into a pink silk moire bag and everything else was boxed and carefully labelled. All the boxes and bags were then bundled into the back of the van, along with Nina and Rose. We pulled down the shutters, climbed into the cab with Gerald and drove off. The journey wasn't without incident, however. Turning down a narrow alleyway, we suddenly found our passage blocked by a large truck reversing towards us. For a few dreadful moments we were convinced it was a heist and that they were going to force us out of the van and steal the clothes. Fortunately, it really was just a garbage truck doing its usual round!

Finally we arrived at the safety of Clarence House, we got everything out of the van, up the stairs and into this tiny little room, right at the top of the building. Just as we were taking the dresses out of the bags and hanging them on the rail, we happened to glance out of the window and spotted builders on the roof right beside us, all peering in. We were really worried and, just as we did at Brook Street, instantly drew all the curtains.

Opposite Finally the dress was finished and we carefully packed it in tissue paper, ready to transport to Clarence House. We had also made a special hanger for it and a little, heart-shaped pot-pourri bag, made out of the dress fabric.

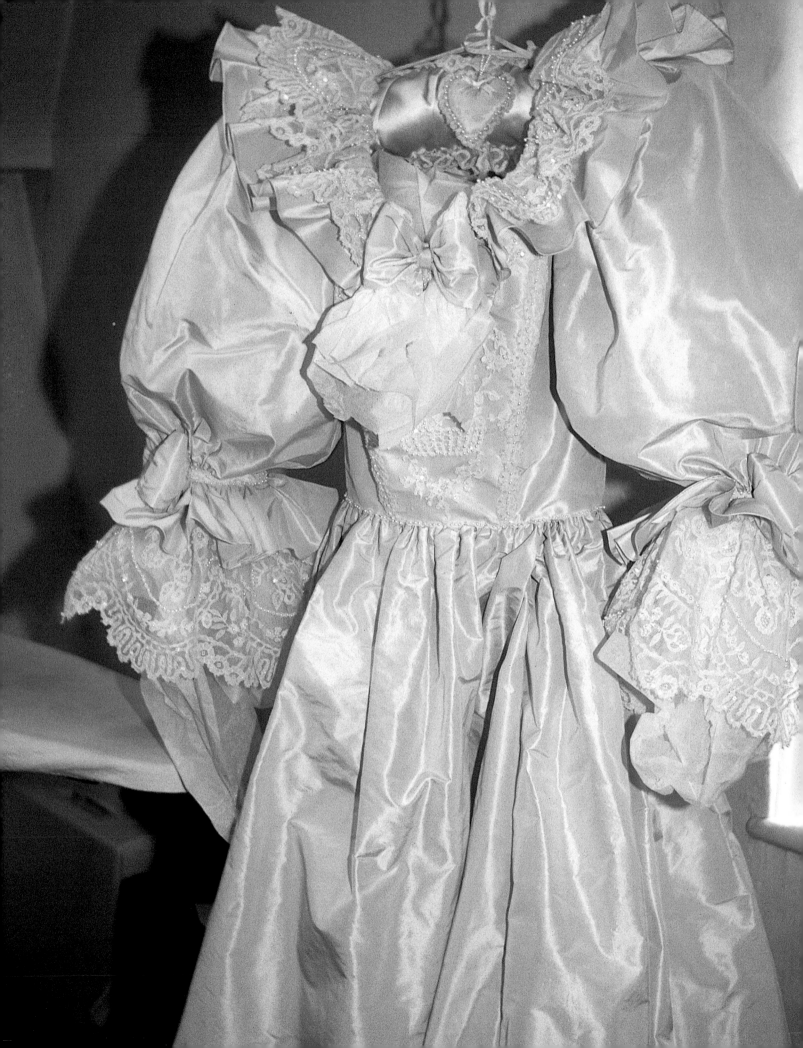

That royal wedding dress had an enormous impact on wedding fashion. The saying goes that imitation is the sincerest form of flattery and the dress certainly proved popular. Immediately people were trying to copy it. But we had decided right from the start that we were going to make it as difficult as possible for anybody to copy. We made the design extremely complex, and there was so much detail with all the lace, sequins and pearls.

Nevertheless, some quite good lookalikes were made – and quickly. It is extraordinary to think that as Diana was walking down the aisle in that gown, there was somebody in a West End studio copying it, sketching it and cutting it out. The first copy was in one of the Oxford Street stores by the very next morning.

Wedding dresses in that period had tended to be quite starchy and formal – very traditional, "A" line and made of white satin. There was no real magic or sense of fairytale, and that was what we had wanted to create. The fact that we made the dress in ivory was different too and started a whole trend in non-white wedding dresses, not only in ivory but also in other shades.

We are amazed when we think of the number of people who have queued and queued, people who have paid to see this gown. It has toured the world and has raised millions and millions of pounds for various charities. If any dress has ever earned its keep, it must surely be Princess Diana's wedding gown.

Right and overleaf Diana's finished wedding dress, complete with the shoes, parasol and one of the bridesmaid's dresses.

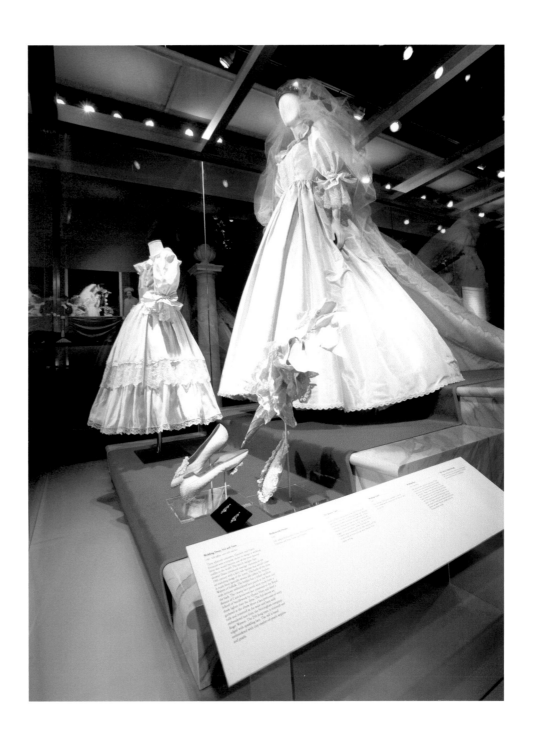

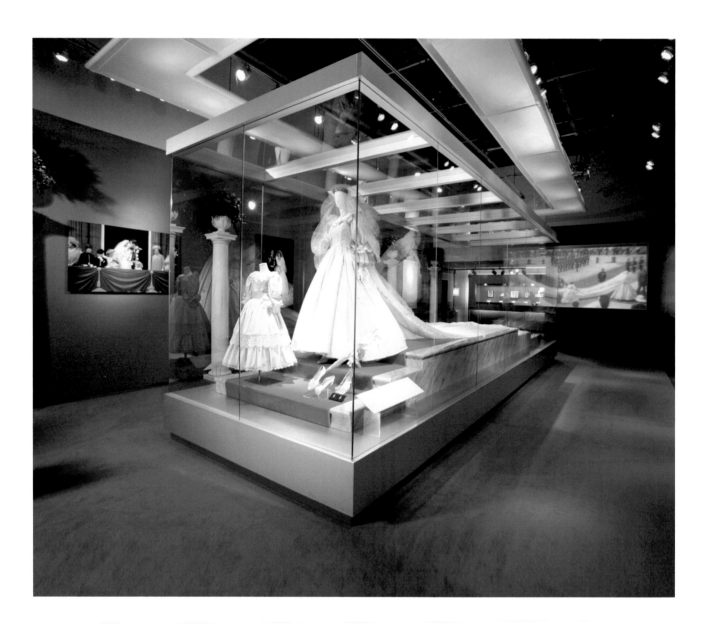

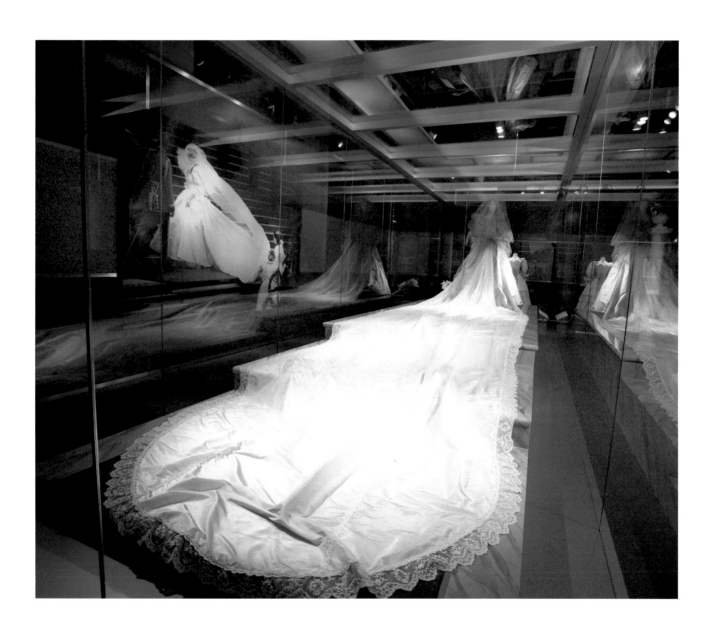

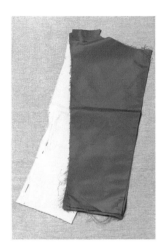
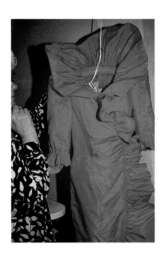

THE PINK DRESS

Two days before the wedding, there was to be a grand ball at Buckingham Palace for the guests who had flown in from around the world to celebrate the wedding. For many, this would be their first glimpse of the new royal bride to be.

Diana wanted to look ultraglamorous for this big event, and by that stage we knew she had the figure of a top model, and was growing more confident by the day. Together with her, we plotted to create a head-turning dress that no-one would expect or forget. We decided on a shocking pink creation in silk taffeta with plunge neckline, body-hugging silhouette and crossover skirt that was slashed to the thigh. She looked like a goddess and she knew it!

As she entered the royal ballroom, heads turned and people audibly gasped – here was a totally different Diana, no longer the shy nursery teacher peering from beneath her fringe, but a glamorous Princess ready to take her place in history. She totally stole the show!

Above right and left A sample of the fabric used for the pink dress. Rose (just seen) standing next to the final piece.
Opposite The original sketch of the dress.

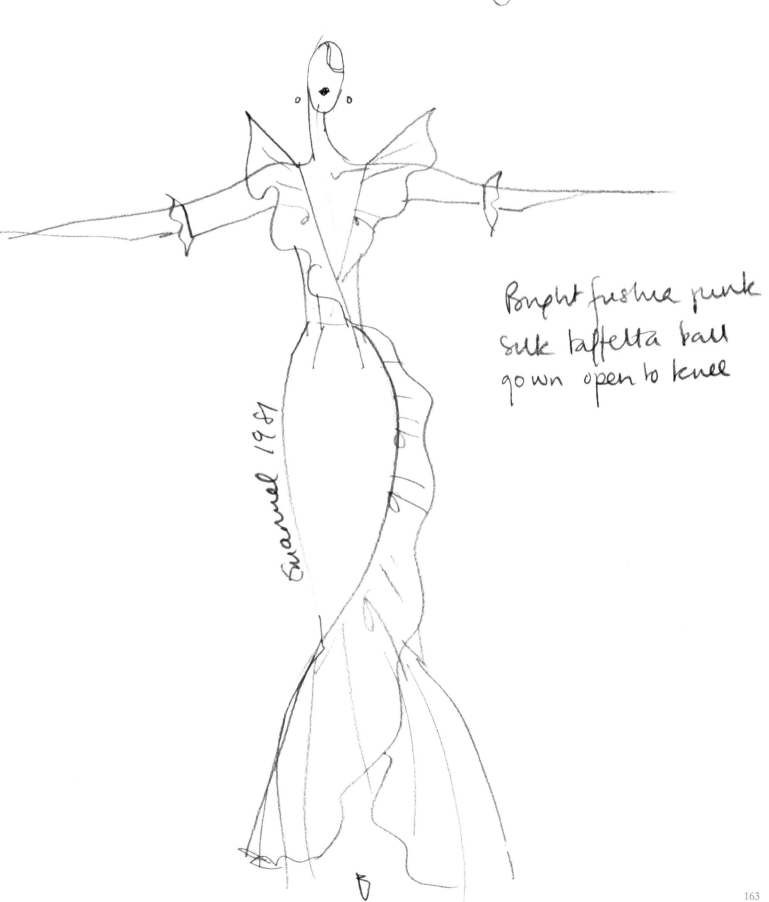

Ball on July 27th
Buck House

Bright fushia punk
silk taffetta ball
gown open to knee

Emanuel 1981

163

EMBARGO

NOT TO BE PUBLISHED, BROADCAST ON RADIO OR TELEVISION, NOR TRANSMITTED OVERSEAS BEFORE 10:35 A.M. ON WEDNESDAY JULY 29th 1981

THE LADY DIANA SPENCER'S WEDDING DRESS

The Wedding Dress is made of ivory pure silk taffeta and old lace, hand-embroidered with tiny mother-of-pearl sequins and pearls. The bodice is fitted and boned with a wide frill around the gently curved neckline, and intricately embroidered lace panels on the front and back. The sleeves are full and gathered into a taffeta frill at the elbow, with an elaborately embroidered lace flounce underneath. Another lace flounce surrounds the neckline, with a taffeta bow to match those on the sleeves. The skirt of the dress is full, worn over a crinoline petticoat consisting of many layers of ivory tulle, and is trimmed around the waist and hem with embroidered lace. The sweeping train, 25 feet long and detachable, is trimmed and edged with the same sparkling lace.

With OLD lace, NEW fabric and a tiara BORROWED from the family collection, there was only one essential missing. A small BLUE bow was sewn into the waistband and the dress was complete. A tiny horseshoe crafted by Douglas Buchanan, made of 18 carat yellow gold and studded with white diamonds, was also sewn into the dress for good luck.

VEIL AND JEWELLERY

Her veil of ivory silk tulle, spangled with thousands of tiny hand-embroidered mother-of-pearl sequins, is held in place by the Spencer Family diamond tiara. Lady Diana is also wearing diamond drop earrings lent by her mother.

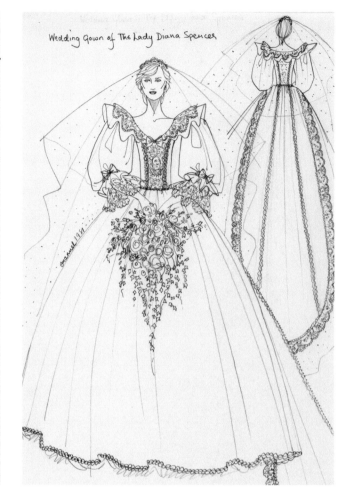

Wedding Gown of The Lady Diana Spencer

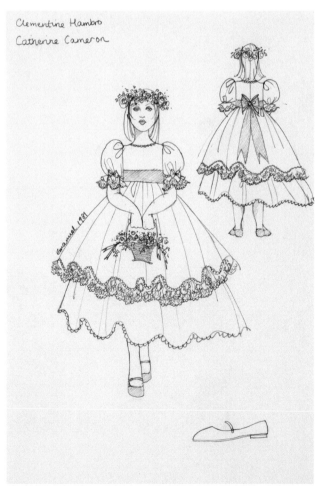

Clementine Hambro
Catherine Cameron

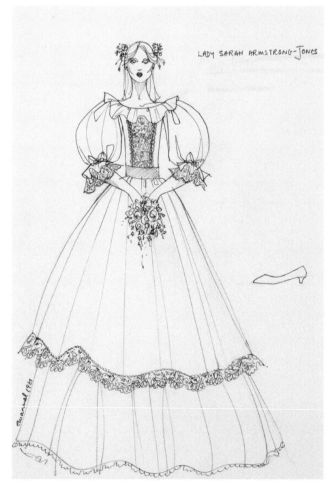

LADY SARAH ARMSTRONG-JONES

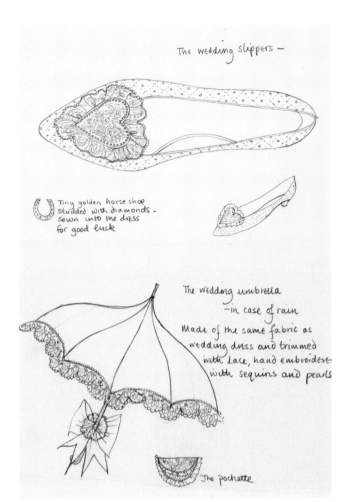

The wedding slippers —

Tiny golden horse shoe studded with diamonds – sewn into the dress for good luck

The wedding umbrella
— in case of rain
Made of the same fabric as wedding dress and trimmed with lace, hand embroidered with sequins and pearls

The pochette

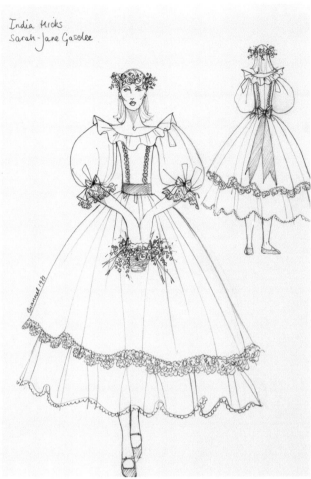

India Hicks
Sarah-Jane Gaselee

THE EMBARGO

Having successfully kept the dress secret for all those months, we wanted to make sure that when the time came the press would have all the facts for accurate reports. So the weekend before the wedding, we locked ourselves away in the studio at Brook Street, with Caroline, to put together the release for the wedding day. We photocopied for hours and hours, then had to deliver boxes full of the finished press release to the Press Office at Buckingham Palace, with "embargo" stamped boldly in red. The embargo was timed to expire when Diana was first seen in the dress on the day itself.

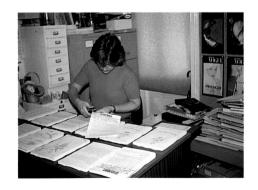

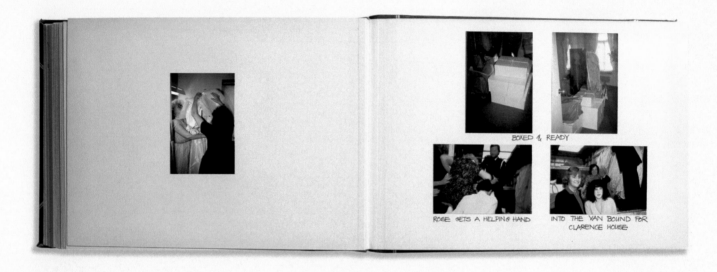

Above and opposite Some of the final photographs from the album, taken on the last few days before the wedding, show us getting the dress wrapped and padded with tissue paper, ready for its journey to Clarence House, where Diana was to get dressed on the morning of her wedding.

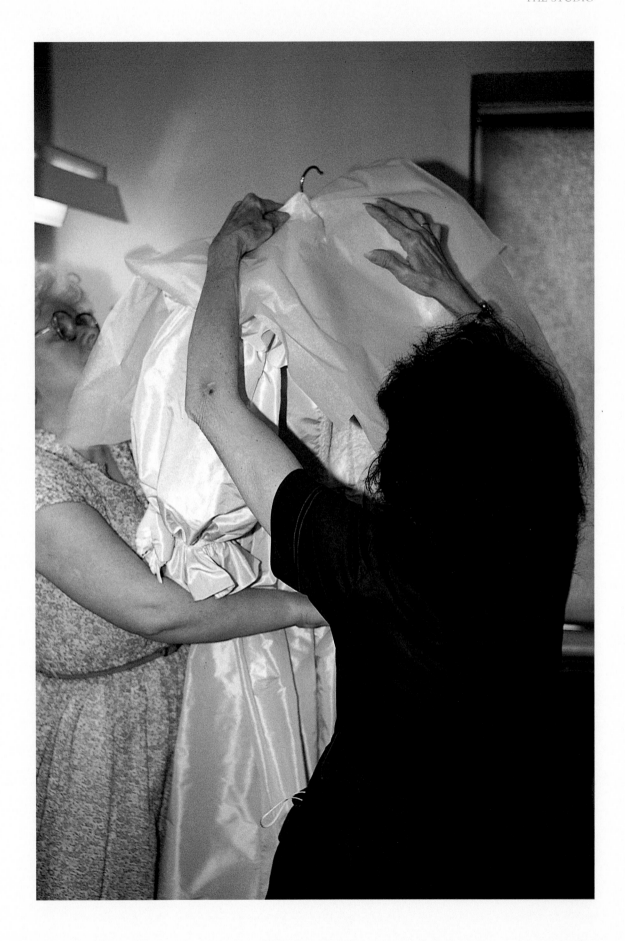

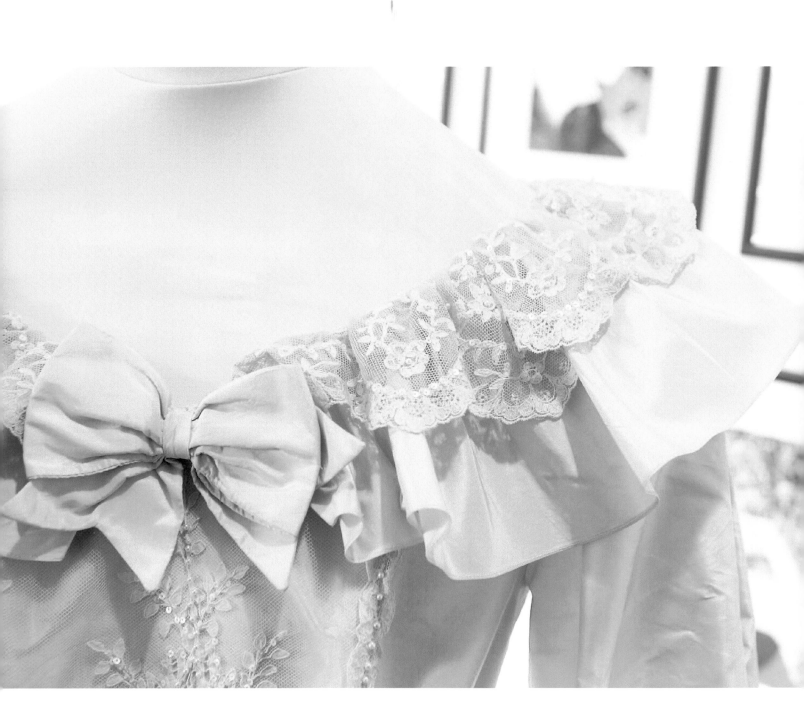

A DRESS FOR MADAME TUSSAUDS

Opposite The replica dress for Madame Tussauds. It has often been asserted that this was a back-up dress. In fact, it was not and was certainly never worn by Diana; it was made specially for display and although it copies the original in most respects, the train was less than half the length of the real one.

Just as we were getting close to completing months of hard work on the dress, we received a phone call from Madame Tussauds, asking us for a duplicate gown. We immediately called the Press Office at Buckingham Palace to ask them to confirm the request. "Well, Mr Emanuel, you know it's for British tourism…", they replied.

Even leaving aside the time constraints, we didn't know if we had enough fabric. Fortunately for us, we discovered that Tussauds had a very limited area in which to display the gown, so instead of making a twenty-five foot train – we knew we wouldn't have time to embroider it – we made one about twelve foot long.

Of course, rather than fitting the dress to a live body we had to fit it to a wax mannequin, which was not even like working with a dressmaker's dummy. When the mannequin arrived, it looked like something out of *ET* – it had no eyes, no mouth and no hair. Tussauds explained to us that only the parts of their models that are on display are made of wax; whatever is hidden is made of plaster. So we were quizzed about the neckline. We suggested they just make it all out of wax, but were told this was impossible. Finally, we said, "Well make it strapless." And so they asked, "Are you going to do a strapless dress for Lady Diana?"

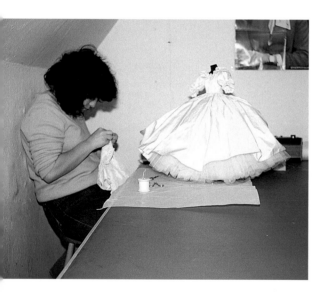

With enormous relief on completing the major work on the dress, the bridesmaid dresses and the Tussauds replica, we still had a small amount of silk remaining. So feeling confident that we were now in the home straight, we decided that it would be great fun to make a miniature of the wedding dress and a matching bridesmaid dress. We knew that previous royal gowns had been exhibited, and wanted to make something unique and special to complement such an exhibition. Using spare pearls and sequins, we hoped to create a doll-sized copy of the gown that captured the essence of the real thing and which would be fun for the public to perhaps see one day.

Above left and opposite Elizabeth working away on the miniature royal wedding dress. The finished result.

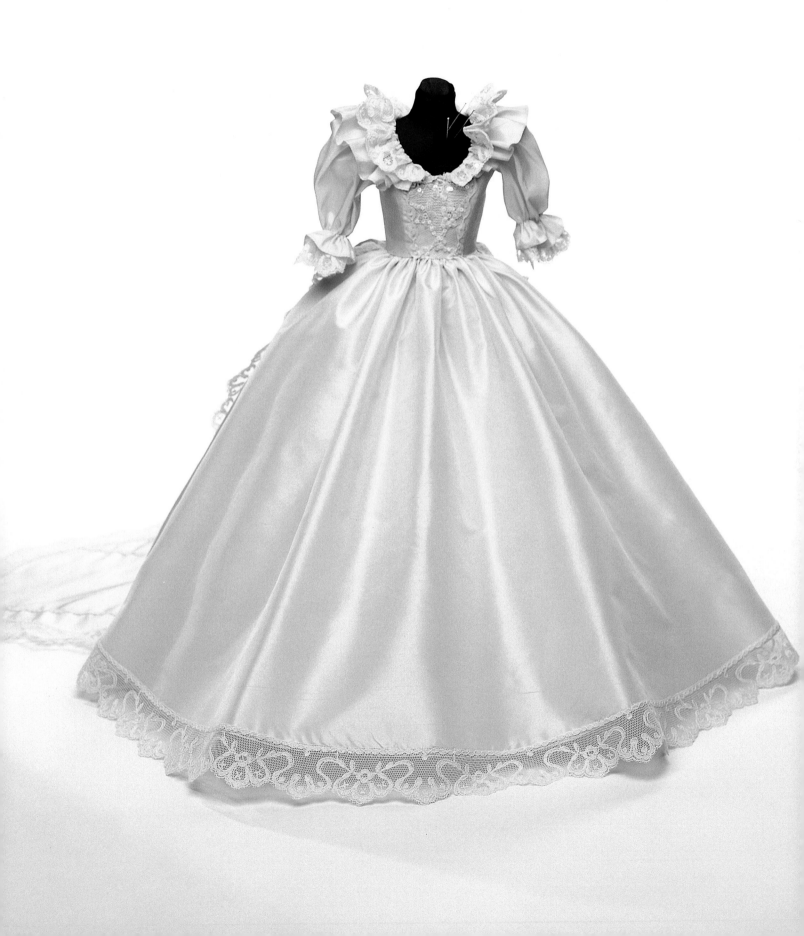

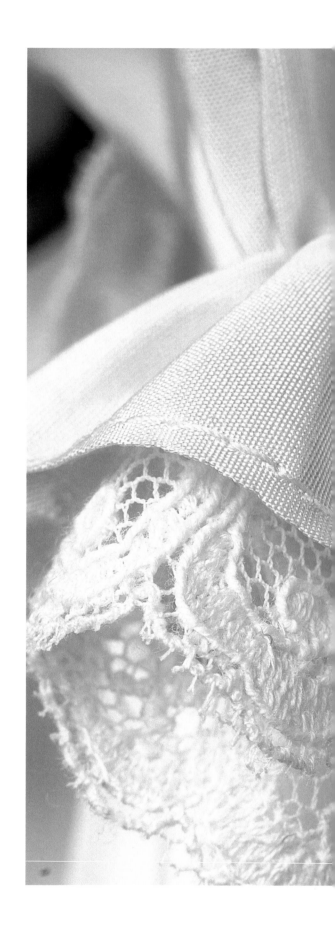

"A special scaled-down version of the lace was included in the miniature dress to preserve the detail and integrity of the full-size dress."

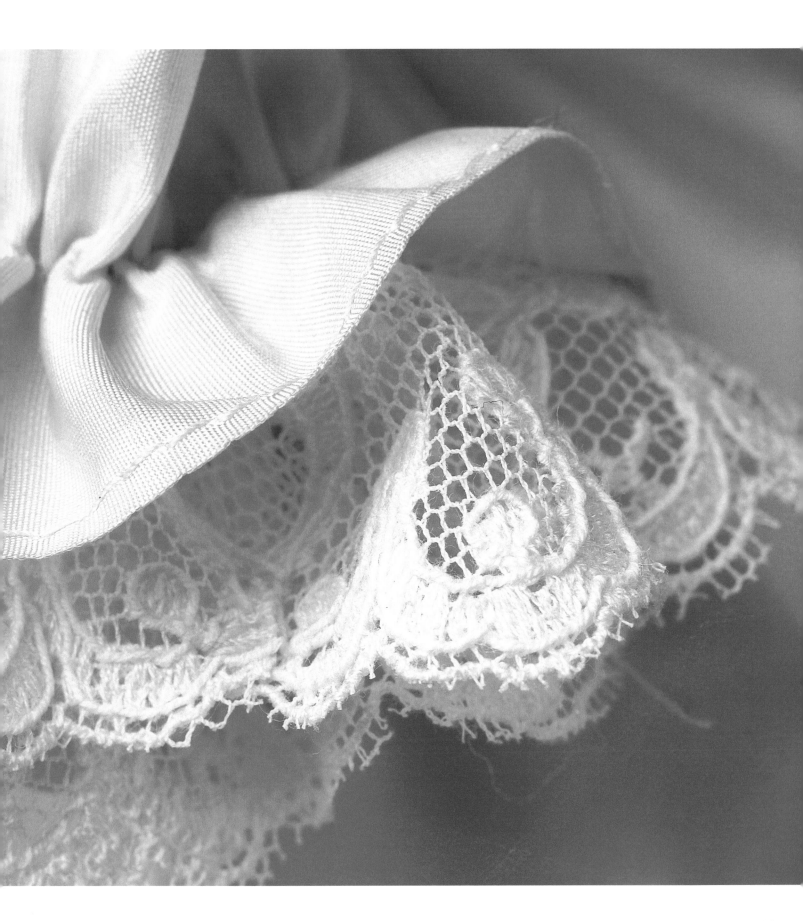

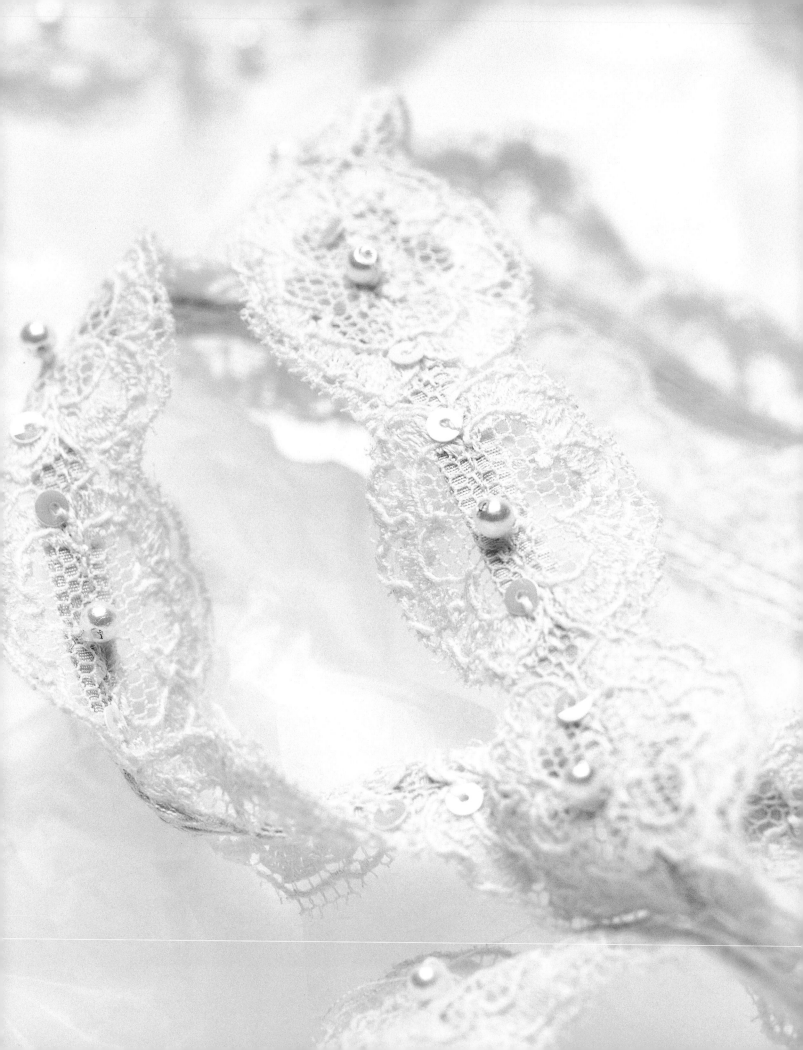

THE WEDDING

The morning of the Royal Wedding finally arrived and it was an early start for us – there was still a lot to do. We had asked a family friend, Wally, to drive us from our family home in Knightsbridge to Clarence House. Both he and his wife were very excited that we had been making the dress, and Wally was thrilled to be able to drive us at the start of this momentous day. (He had been very ill and died only a couple of months after the wedding, so we were really glad that we had been able to share that moment together.)

As we drove up the Mall, crowds of people were already gathered on either side of the road behind safety barriers. They didn't know who we were but were already screaming with excitement – clearly something was beginning to happen, though there were still several hours to go before they might hope to glimpse the bride.

When we arrived at Clarence House, we found Diana relaxed in a white towelling dressing gown and having her hair and make-up done, while her bridesmaids watched television. Through the window in her dressing room we watched the huge crowd building up and could hear them all shouting. We could also see guards going past, marching down The Mall towards St. Paul's, and could hear the sound of trumpet fanfares. And then, turning our heads, we could watch it all happening on the television. The scene switched to commentator Judith Chalmers, who was trying to predict what the wedding dress would look like. And we were thinking, "We know!" It was a very strange experience to be watching these momentous events unfolding on the screen, knowing that we were playing an important part in what was taking place. Despite the fact that it was such an important occasion, and we were all really nervous, the atmosphere at Clarence House that morning felt surprisingly relaxed. There was an ad for Cornetto and Diana was singing along as we all had our orange juice and biscuits. We we were having a great time!

But, of course, it wasn't all drinks, biscuits, television and laughter – we had an important job to do and it involved more organization than the biggest fashion show we had ever done. The whole thing was run like a military operation. We had clipboards, we had guys telling everyone that at so many hundred hours, Lady Diana should get into the dress; at so many hundred hours, she should descend to the carriage, and so on. We were constantly moving from one room to another to keep a check on things. In fact, at one stage Elizabeth was running along a corridor when she bumped into the Queen Mother. She must have been making too much noise because Her Majesty gave her a rather stern look!

"There were nerves and excitement for us, but actually we were focused on work; we had a job to do. It was like the biggest fashion show in the world we would ever do."

As at any photo shoot or fashion show, the bride had to have her hair and make-up done before putting on her dress. In a way, part of our job was to calm the girls down. Diana was full of energy and very excited, but fortunately, Barbara Daly, the make-up artist, was very calming as well as very professional. Next, Kevin, her hairdresser, had to style her hair. (Meanwhile, his wife was looking after the bridesmaids' hair.)

Timing was crucial: we couldn't afford to be late, but we wanted to leave it until the last possible minute before getting Diana into her gown so that she wasn't standing around in it. Nina was helping us here too. First, Diana had to get into her petticoat, then put on her shoes. And then, finally, we slipped her into the dress. That was an incredibly moving moment! Then, suddenly, Elizabeth asked: "Did you do up the double hook on her petticoat?" The petticoat was an enormous crinoline tulle affair, which we had spent ages trimming very carefully to ensure that it was exactly the right length so that Diana wouldn't trip on it. None of us could remember having done up the hook and we had awful visions of her walking down the aisle and the petticoat coming adrift! There was only one thing to be done: David, dressed in his frockcoat, had to get underneath all Diana's skirts to check the hook. As he resurfaced, the door to the room opened and Diana coolly asked, "David, have you met the Queen Mother?" She wanted to privately wish Diana good luck and to check that she was alright.

Once Diana was dressed, we checked that the children were ready too. The very last thing to be done was to put the bridesmaids' flower circlets on their heads and hand them their baskets of flowers. And then Diana and her party were finally ready to go.

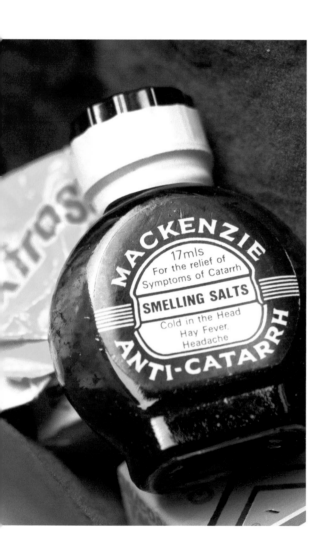

Above The contents of Elizabeth's handbag.
Opposite Our timetable for the day.

Even getting Diana to the door of Clarence House took some time. We had to walk through the house, then down the grand staircase and at this stage we had to fold the enormous train almost like you would fold sheets. And then we waited, all lined up on the stairs, for what seemed like an age for the carriage to arrive.

In her handbag, Elizabeth had the foresight to have a bottle of smelling salts and some sugar tablets in case Diana felt faint, but she didn't need either. Now that all the preparations were complete, she seemed very relaxed, and only Elizabeth needed the sugar tablets. Diana was also great with the bridesmaids – constantly reassuring and calming. Then, at last, the carriage pulled up and Diana's father, Earl Spencer, was at the foot of the stairs greeting everybody.

The glass carriage in which Diana was to travel was made in 1910 and was also used to carry HM The Queen to her wedding with the Duke of Edinburgh, as well as for many other royal weddings. On the outside it looks large, but inside, the seats, which are beautifully upholstered and buttoned, are quite small. We had rehearsed getting Diana into the carriage once before at The Royal Mews, but without Earl Spencer, who was quite a big man. Once Diana was seated beside her father, we had to fold up twenty-five feet of silk-taffeta train and concertina it inside the carriage, making sure that Diana was comfortable for the journey.

As the doors opened and the carriage finally pulled away, we could hear what sounded like a collective intake of breath from the crowd, then the applause commenced.

7:30 David, Liz, Nina & Rose leave Ovington St

8:00 " " " " arrive Clarence House

9:15 Gerald & Caroline to Brook St. to collect Mr Hoey & George

9:15 Nina & Rose leave Clarence House in coach for St. Paul's

9:30 BBC to Brook Street

10:37 David & Liz leave Clarence House for St. Paul's (Captain Alistair Aird's car)

11:00 Wedding

12:30 David & Liz to Buckingham Palace (Everyone else back to Brook St.)

12:30 BBC leave Brook St.

2:00 David & Liz collected from B.P.

2:30 ITN to Brook St. — Nina & Rose

4:00 Cindy, Caroline, Charles Gerald to IMG.

3:00 Press Conference at IMG

5:30 M. Tussaud's collect from Brook St.

6:30?/7:00? David & Liz to M.T.

8:30 Dinner

10:30 The Gardens

"AS DIANA LEFT CLARENCE HOUSE AND THE GLASS CARRIAGE TURNED INTO THE MALL, YOU COULD SEE HER SMILING BEHIND HER VEIL, AND THEN A SEQUIN CAUGHT THE LIGHT AND SPARKLED, WHICH WAS SOMETHING WE HAD NEVER SEEN BEFORE — SEQUINS ON A VEIL. I COULD ALSO SEE THE ELEGANT FULL SLEEVES ON THE DRESS, AND KNEW THERE AND THEN THAT THIS WAS GOING TO BE A VERY GRAND DRESS — VERY EXCITING AND ORIGINAL, AND PROBABLY NOT WHAT ANYONE WAS EXPECTING. THE ONLY THING I KNEW IN ADVANCE WAS THAT IT WOULD BE A VERY LONG TRAIN, AS WE AT THE BBC HAD SEEN THE REHEARSAL IN ST PAUL'S. THAT DAY DIANA LOOKED WONDERFUL — IT REALLY WAS THE YOUNG ROMANTIC FAIRYTALE IMAGE OF CINDERELLA ON HER WEDDING DAY."

Eve Pollard, BBC Fashion commentator for the Royal Wedding

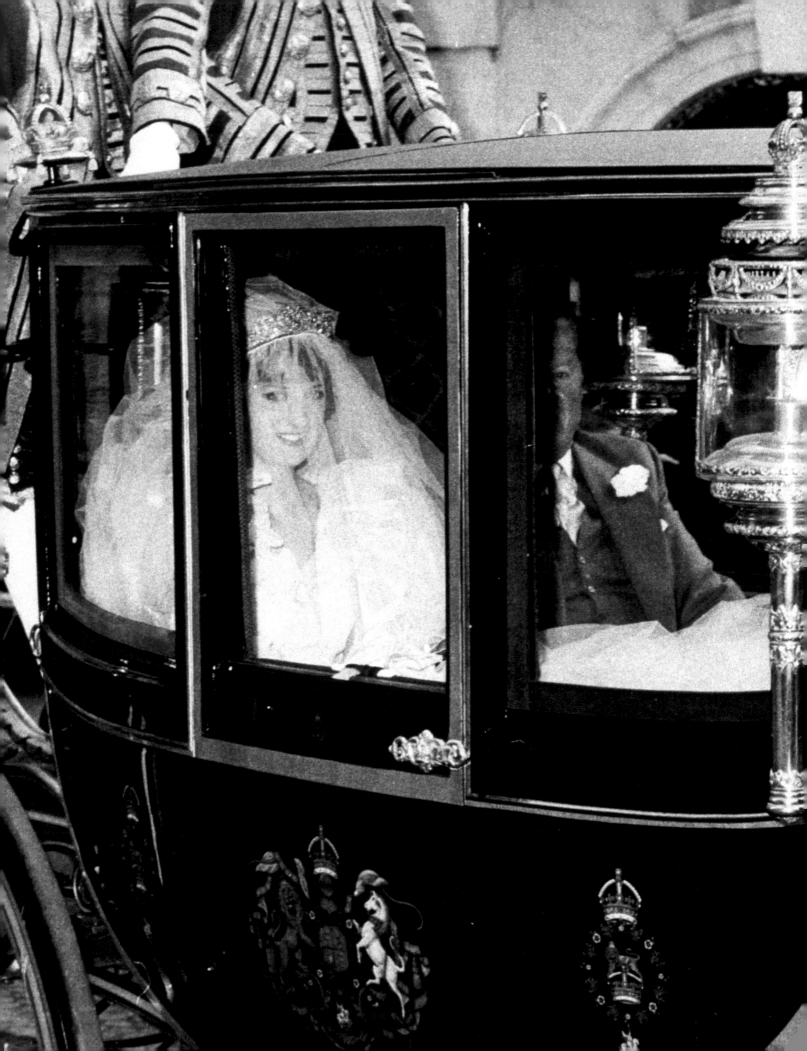

Meanwhile, another car drew up to take us, fast track, with a police escort, through the back streets of London to St. Paul's, so that we could be there, ready and waiting, when Diana arrived. We entered the cathedral through one of the side entrances, and were escorted past the assembled dignatories to the grand pillars at the front, where we had been instructed to wait at the top of the stairs. Never before had St. Paul's seemed so massive to us. Though the cathedral itself was already full of wedding guests, the entrance seemed vast and cavernous as we stood there waiting for the carriage to draw up.

That was probably the only time that either of us felt really nervous that day. Suddenly everything had become very real and here we were, standing at the entrance of the cathedral, while HM The Queen, Prince Philip and the entire Royal family were lined up in all their finery at the top of the red-carpeted aisle to greet the newest member of their family. That's when the reality finally hit home.

And then, we began to hear this applause from the crowd, which gradually grew louder and louder as the carriage drew nearer. There was a moment when this enormous cheer broke out and we realized that Diana had arrived.

"Up till then, it had been such a secret – we were so good at conditioning ourselves to speak to nobody. We didn't breath a word. You couldn't tell your friends, you couldn't discuss anything, and it all had to be held together. But suddenly it became very real and we thought, 'This is it!'"

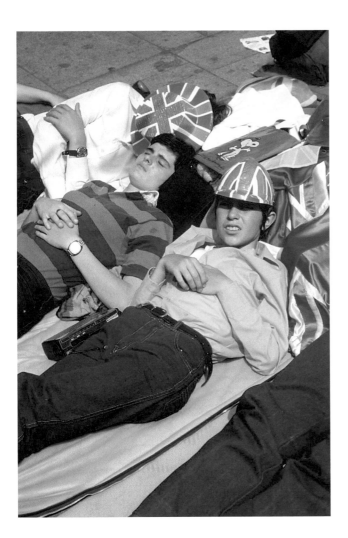

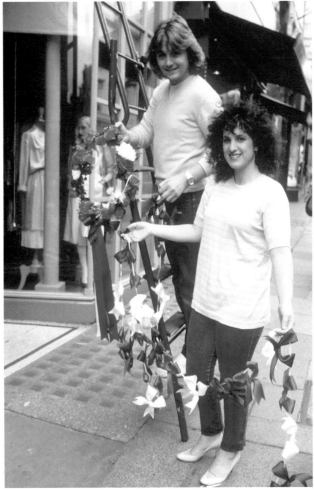

Above left Some of the millions of people who lined the streets and slept out for days to get the best vantage point.
Above right Joining in with the spirit of the occasion, we decided to decorate the outside of Brook Street.

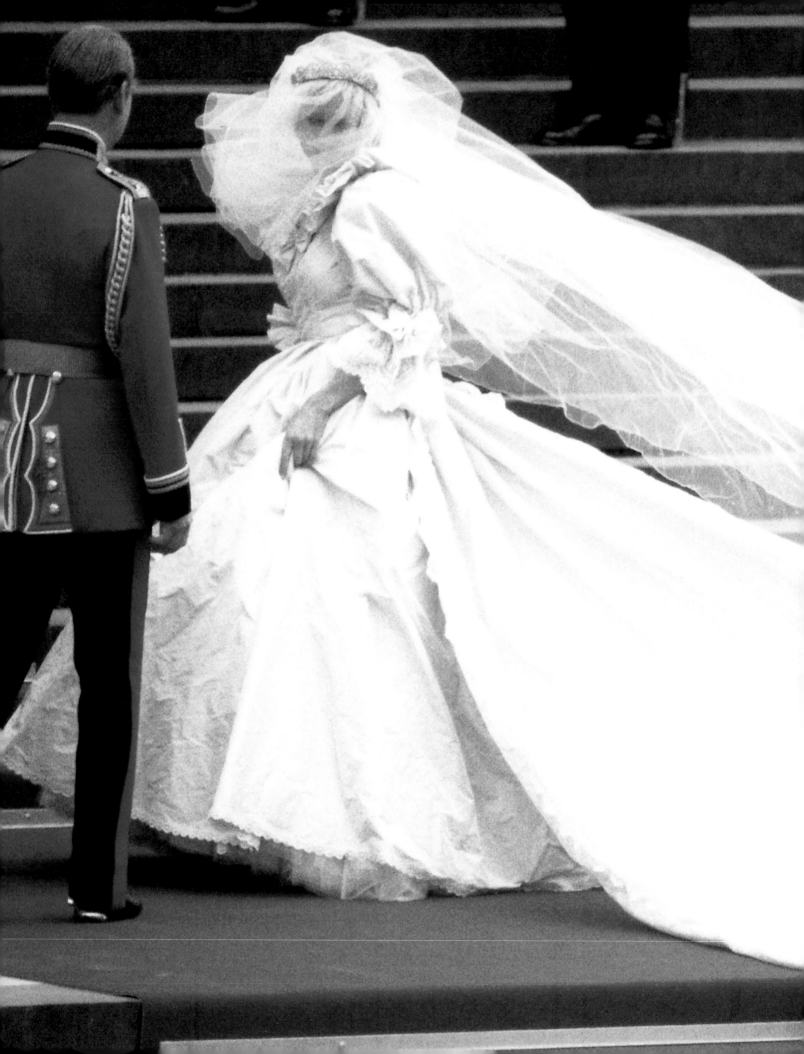

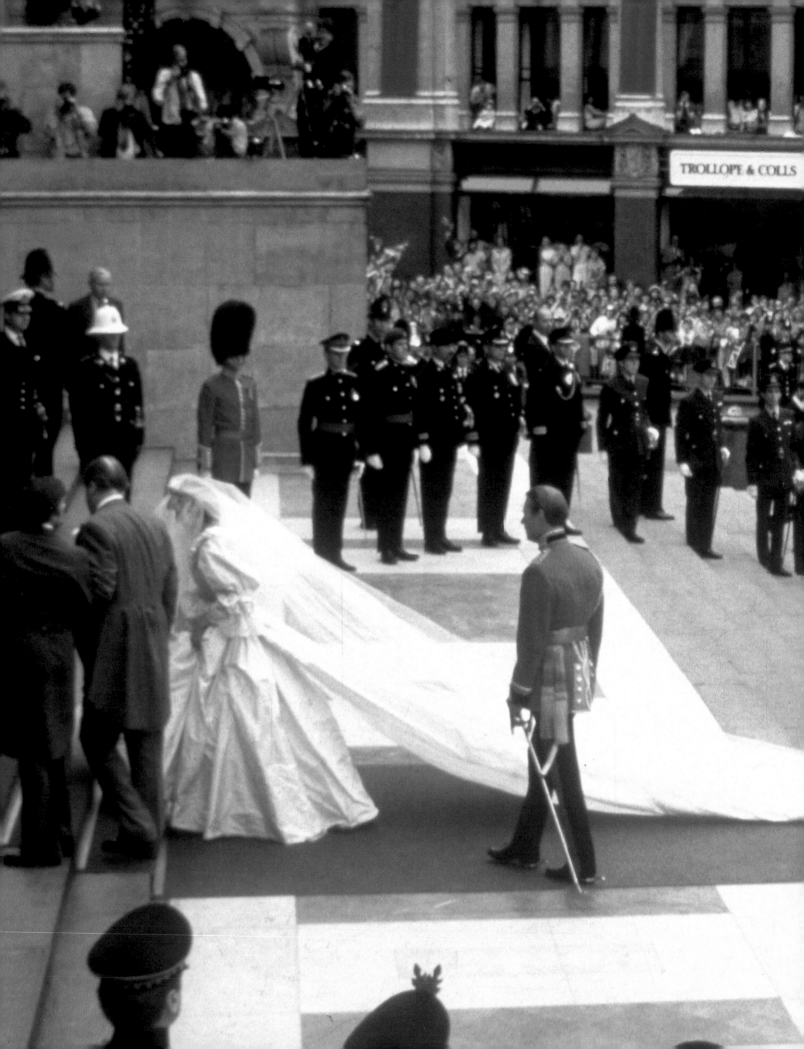

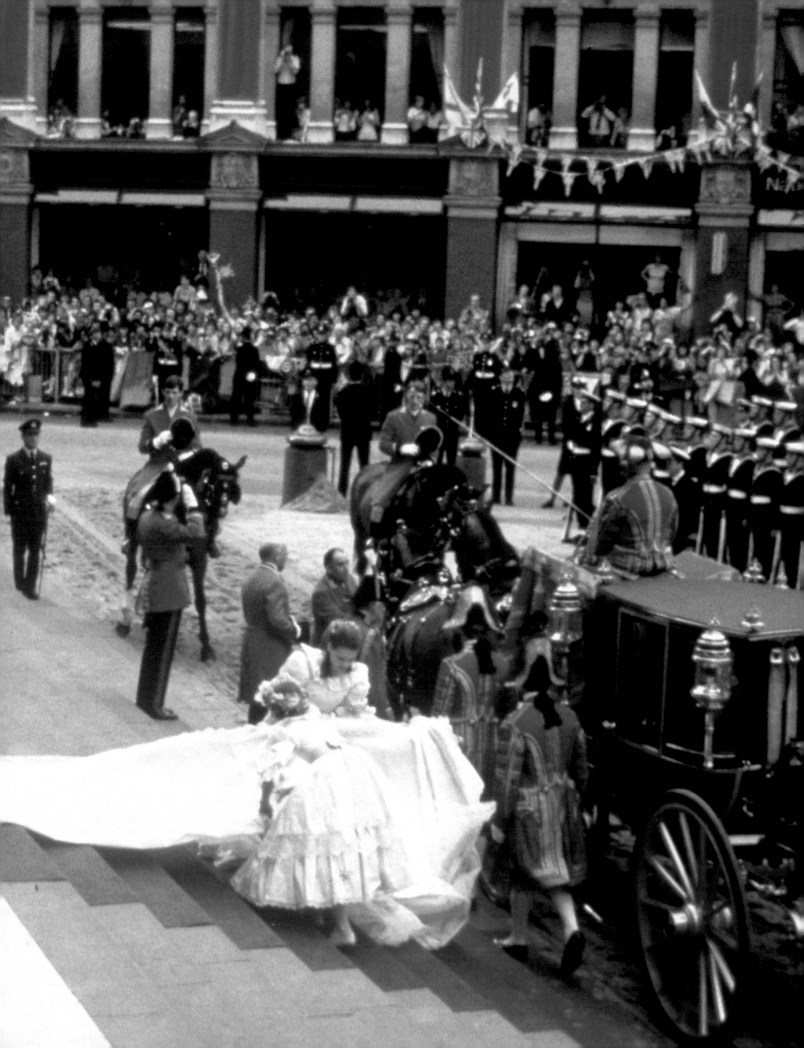

One of the most dramatic moments of the whole wedding was watching Diana alight from the carriage – it was like seeing a butterfly emerge from a chrysalis. As she got out, the train expanded and it just kept on coming and coming and you wondered when it was ever going to end. You could hear the crowd gasp with disbelief that a train that long could come out of a coach so small. Everybody seemed to love that magical moment.

Again, time seemed to stand still as we waited for her to come up the steps – there are a lot of them and there were many photographs taken. Earl Spencer, despite his ill health, escorted his daughter superbly. Unfortunately, as we watched her come towards us, we noticed immediately that the dress had been crushed *en route* and we panicked a bit. "Oh my god, it's creased", Elizabeth whispered. Of course, it had been cramped in the carriage, but we hadn't anticipated that it would look that crumpled.

Nevertheless, the moment that Diana appeared to the world wearing the dress that we had designed for her was such a special moment for us. The gown looked so theatrical, so dramatic and so beautiful. It was every girl's fantasy, fairytale wedding dress. And strangely, its imperfections seemed to make it almost more beautiful.

Opposite However nervous she was feeling inside, Diana appeared perfectly relaxed and blissfully happy on her wedding day. And as was to characterize her public life as the Princess of Wales, she cheerfully made time to chat and smile and put others at their ease. The transformation was complete: the young, naive, even somewhat gauche nursery school teacher had already become a royal princess.

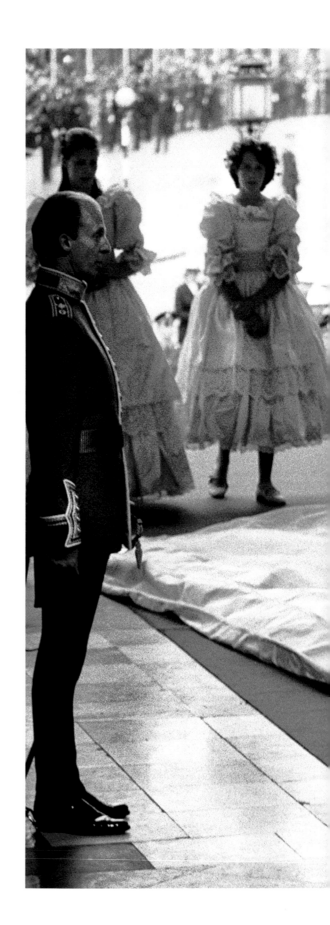

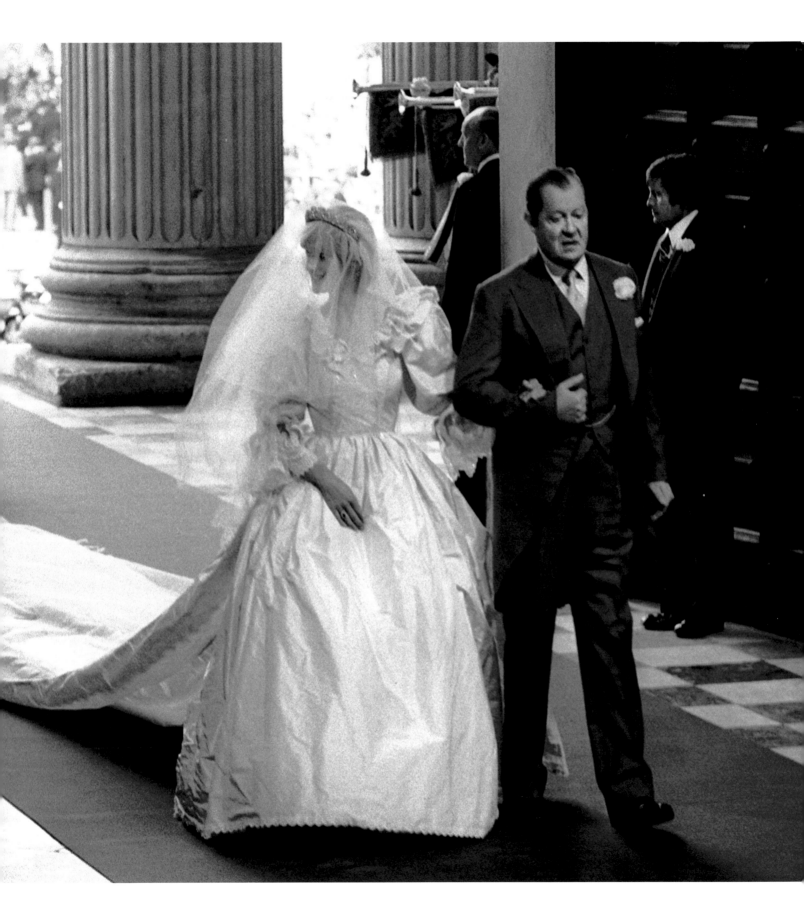

It had been planned that Diana, on cue, would step forward. The cameras would then focus on the stained glass, the flowers, the guests or whatever, while we would spring into action to arrange the dress, the veil, the train and check on the bridesmaids. David, because he is taller, focused his attention on the top of the dress and the veil, while Elizabeth checked the skirt and the back of the dress. We fluffed out Diana's skirts and pulled out all the folds – thankfully they smoothed out straight away. David briefly checked her hair and face, then whispered a few words of encouragement to her. Then she was ready to walk down the aisle with her father, who would hand her to her prince. Meanwhile, we were ushered to our seats and waited for the wedding ceremony to begin.

(When we arrived back at Brook Street later that day, the team was waiting for us in the workroom. Those that weren't at St Paul's had been watching the event on television and told us that, though we had thought we would be off camera, we had been filmed all the time we were making final adjustments to the dress and that the footage had been broadcast to the world.)

Unfortunately, we were seated behind a pillar, so like many of the other assembled guests, we couldn't see much of what was happening. Later, watching the event on video, we could see how wonderful Diana looked and how well the young bridesmaids coped with their immense task of trying to get that train to behave. Just as Kiri te Kanawa began to sing "Let the Bright Seraphim", David received a tap on the shoulder, the signal to exit for the next phase of our working day. This time, we would be waiting for the new Princess of Wales at Buckingham Palace.

Opposite Up until this point, all our work on the dress had been done in secret. As we made the final adjustments to Diana's dress, and tried to straighten out the creases, just before she walked down the aisle on the arm of her father, we little realized that the eyes of the world were watching. David helps Diana with her bouquet, seconds before she begins her journey down the aisle.

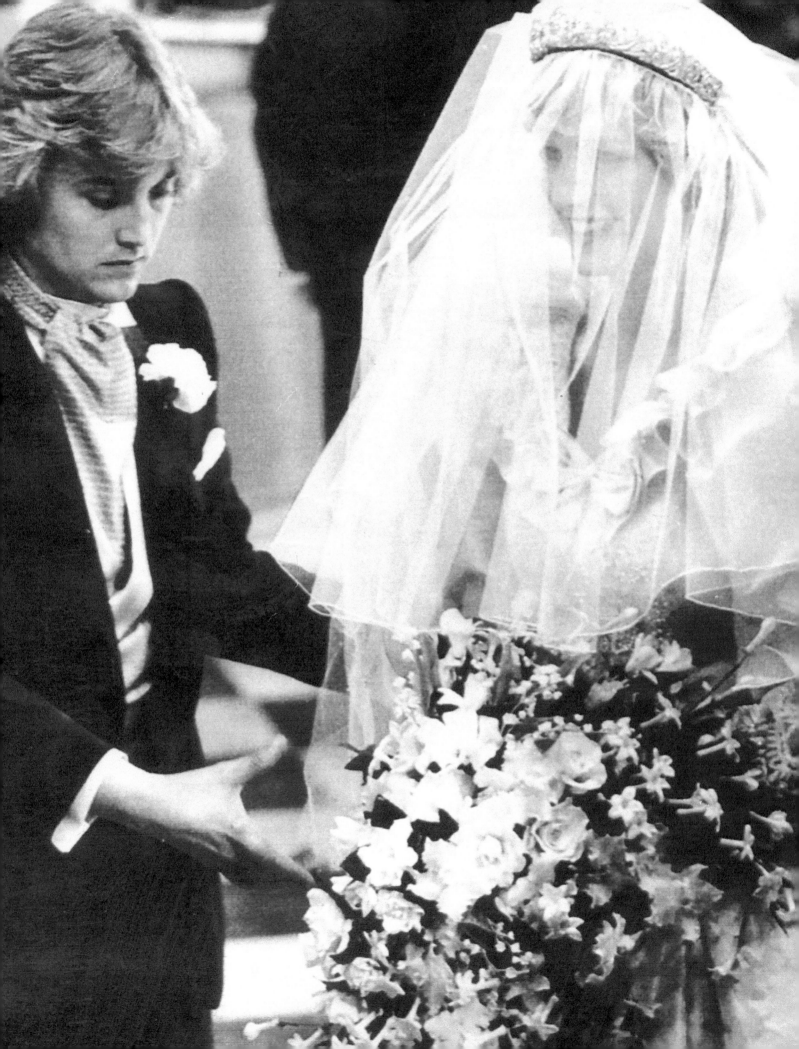

We quietly slipped out of the side entrance, got back into the car, and were driven at great speed through every red light, to Buckingham Palace, once again with a police escort. (Only one person of our team had been permitted to remain behind to attend to Diana and check her appearance after the couple had signed the register, and we decided that Barbara Daly should be there to touch up her make-up.) We had done the fashion show, now was the fashion shoot – only this was not a studio but the Throne Room at Buckingham Palace and there was an awful lot of red velvet everywhere! The assistants of Lord Litchfield, the royal photographer, had already set up all the lights and a stepladder, checked everything and were ready to begin as soon as the newly married couple arrived.

By the time Princess Diana arrived back at the palace, she must have been both physically and emotionally exhausted – she had been under the intensive gaze of millions of people for hours and was now standing in the Throne Room, still holding her huge bouquet. David took the flowers from her, explaining to those present that she needed to rest, and spotting Prince Andrew, who was attired in his wonderful naval officer's uniform, promptly handed the bouquet to him to hold.

It was then, of course, we saw the Royal family in a different light. We realized that, though this had been the grandest of all weddings, and on view to the world, it was, in other ways, much like any other family wedding. Everything had gone well, everyone was happy and now they were having fun, chatting to each other and toasting the happy couple.

It had been an early start and a long and tiring – though incredibly exciting – day for us. We had been at Clarence House, St. Paul's Cathedral

"We pulled it off against all the odds and we will always have happy memories of that day, you know. It was a truly wonderful time."

and at the Throne Room at Buckingham Palace, from where we had a unique vantage point on the famous royal kiss and the millions of people behind the gates. It had been very emotional and very draining. As we finally left the palace, an American journalist came up to us and asked, "OK, kids are you going to retire?" "Retire?", we replied, "We're only just starting our careers, you know!"

Arriving back at Brook Street was wonderful. All the team were there: some had been watching the whole event on the television, while others had been at the wedding at St Paul's. (After the service, Rose and Caroline had to walk back to the studio – crowds filled every street and there was no way anyone could get a taxi that day.) Those who had been watching the events on television at Brook Street were themselves filmed by a BBC camera crew, who were recording their reactions to the broadcast. When we arrived back, everybody was very emotional and we cracked open a couple of bottles of Champagne to celebrate. The team had survived twenty-four-hour security, people rummaging through the bins and journalists offering five-figure sums of money in exchange for any information about the dress. All of our hard work had finally paid off: we had kept the dress a secret for months and now it had been seen by the world, and the world – and, more importantly for us, Diana – had loved it!

But the day was still not over: Rose and Caroline had to take the replica dress to Madame Tussauds, where they dressed the dummy, ready for the crowds to see it the very next day.

After all the months of build-up to the royal wedding and then the excitement of the day itself, we understandably felt somewhat deflated by

July 30th 1981

Your Royal Highness,

David and I just cannot really put into words how happy and proud we feel this morning — and now your phone call has just made our day.

Now that the immediate pressure has died down we have a chance to say thankyou for this greatest of all honours — making your wedding dress, which was for both of us the commission of a life-time. It is something about which we will be able to tell our children the time that the girls began to make their way home. And then the phone rang. It was late enough for us to wonder who on earth would be calling us at that hour. It was Diana! We didn't know where she was, but she was calling us to thank us for making her wedding dress and said she wanted to tell us how beautiful it was and how wonderful she had felt wearing it.

That was the sort of sweet, kind and thoughtful girl Diana was. She had been married only a few hours and yet she had thought to call to let us know how much the dress had meant to her. That call really made our day. It made it complete. It was wonderful!

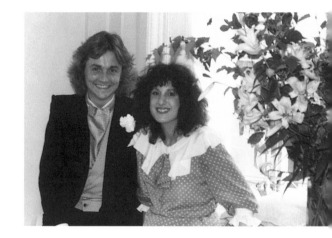

Opposite and above right Our thank you letter to Diana, written the day after the wedding. We were so blessed to have been given such a unique commission. Celebrating back at Brook Street.

In the weeks following the wedding, the postbags at Brook Street were crammed full of congratulatory letters from all corners of the world. Some were simply addressed to "The Emanuels, London", others to "The Emanuels, Buckingham Palace"! We were totally over-whelmed and helped by Caroline, our dutiful PA, we spent many months answering every single letter.

However, the letters that meant most were those from Diana herself. Despite her ever increasing hectic royal schedule, she never failed to take the time to personally handwrite a thank-you note.

Opposite Although Princess Diana and Prince Charles apparently received more than 11,000 wedding presents, she still took the time to write personally to thank us for the album we had made for her to commemorate the making of her wedding dress.

October 10th
1981.

Dear Liz.

What a truly
wonderful surprise I got
when a huge & heavy
parcel arrived for us!

A million heartfelt
thanks to such special
people for giving us
a particularly touching
wedding present.

What a lovely idea &

it goes without saying
how treasured it will
always be, all those
memories ..... phew!

Being up here for so
long is very spoiling but
glorious, especially as
London & I don't see
eye to eye!

I do hope it won't be
too long before I see you
both again, but until
then many many thanks
for giving us the memorable
album - I can't tell
you how pos it brought

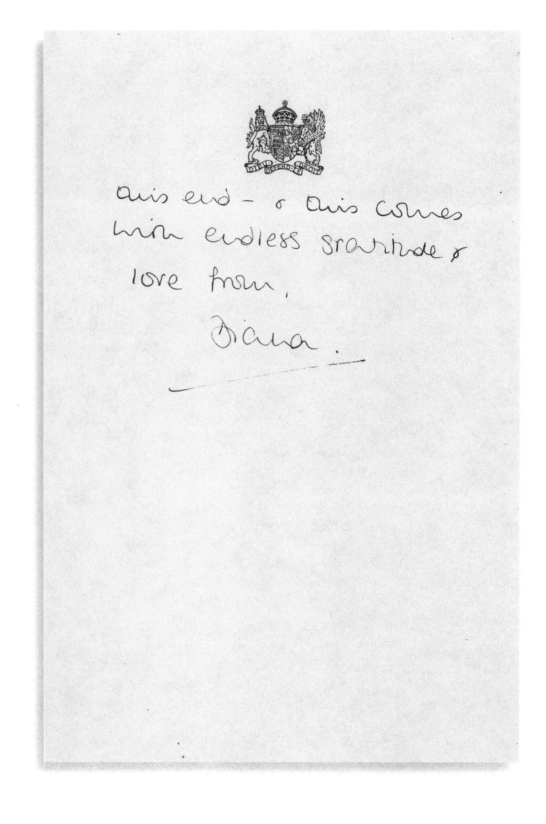

this end — & this comes
with endless gratitude &
love from,

Diana.

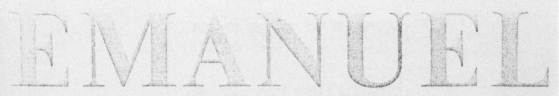

EMANUEL

DAVID EMANUEL   ELIZABETH EMANUEL

TO: The Hon Mrs Peter Shand-Kydd   6 August 1981
      Ardencaple
      Isle of Seil
      By Oban
      Argyll
      Scotland

I N V O I C E

H R H The Princess of Wales' wedding dress, made
of ivory pure silk taffeta and old lace, hand-
embroidered with sequins and pearls, with fitted
boned bodice, large sleeves and full skirt, worn
over large tulle petticoat, Long detachable
train edged in embroidered lace, and ivory silk
tulle veil hand-embroidered with sequins.

Bridesmaids' dresses for Lady Sarah Armstrong-
Jones, India Hicks, Sarah-Jane Gaselee, Catherine
Cameron and Clementine Hambro.

TOTAL 1,000 GUINEAS   £1,050:00

LESS DEPOSIT PAID 4 JUNE 1981   £ 500:00

TOTAL TO PAY   £ 550:00

ARDENCAPLE
ISLE OF SEIL
BY OBAN
ARGYLL.
BALVICAR 213   14/8/81.

Dear Liz and David,

Can I add another set of mammoth congratulations to you both. IT was Superb - in fact So Superlative, that the English language doesn't have such descriptive words - Also many, many thanks for all your help in achieving it - The Bride was always so happy and confident with her visits to you -

Yours Sincerely,

Frances Shand Kydd

Opposite After the wedding, we received an avalanche of letters from members of the public, whose enthusiastic response to the dress was quite overwhelming. We were also inundated with requests from prospective clients, who were all desperate for a dress from the Emanuels. We vowed never to make a copy of the dress for anyone.

yours,

cases!

Leicester where there are
one is not used to the arr

nking you in anticipation of your rep
this opportunity to congratulate you
s of Wales' wedding dress. It was bea
unexpected design.

Yours sincerely,

Gardner.

Geraldine Gardner (Mrs)

11th August, 1981.

Dear Miss Weüzell,

Thank you so much for your kind **letter** to
David and Elizabeth - it was very thoughtful
of you to write and they appreciate it very
much.

Best wishes,

Dear Mr and Mrs

Dear Mr. and Mrs.
congratulations to
simply recieve on
designed and hir e
Spender and hir c
Wedding —
must both be
creations gav
guests at
Who saw

Dear and Elizabe
Just a note to say that
looked out of this world.
Beautiful, gorgeous, wonder
marvellous, fantastic are not
enough words to discribe how s
inthe dress you designed, you m
very proud.
Please give my congratulations to
Missetzis.
From one very proud English pe

Yours faithfully

Sarah Webzell

Miss Sarah Web

POST CARD

DENNIS Productions

ROYAL MARRIAGE 14p

to 26,Brook Sṭ
DAVID + ELIZABETH.
EMANUEL W I
The Royal Wedding Dre
Designers.
LONDON
W1

Printed & Published by E. T. W. DENNIS & SONS LTD., SCARBOROUGH.
Photocolour
90

---

g DIANA Wedding
is the most
beautiful dress she ever
been in my life - & I'm
ever likely to see ever
again - and the bridesmaid
dresses were
enchanting.
Good Luck!
from Freda

am
am sure

---

w you have the ex
er's wedding dress, w
et until the day. But I, a
cussing it, (but perhaps no
e been greatly worried by
pers of completely off-th
the black dress you ma

urely these styles do
modest unspoilt yout
strength and charm
at large with her
(as at the Oper
of the world"
of course b
reserved f

So I, and a
her to follow h
mple of decorum
day of her
for

David & Elizabeth,

Thank you for your part
in giving so much joy, beauty
d perfection to so many people
in one day.

An old age pensioner.

LAMBOURN 71503

Madam,

Dear Ly,
Teal ya all so much
fo th lovlu dress and all you
did for S.J. The wdo day was
so lovbcl and th dress and th
otlers could not have been
more forlcd. We have been
watchin th video and th colou
wos perfecth toucly in th
Cathedral - especiall, in all whot
Also thah ya so much fo
taily and silk worms.
I will did on you
I left forgotte

Ha
And
to thank

"We both feel so honoured that Diana chose us to design that dress. She could have played safe and gone to one of the more established designers, but instead she chose us, and we were newcomers, and it changed our lives completely. Would we alter anything? Absolutely not. That dress was perfect for her for that time. Everything about that day was just so unique and there will never be another day, or another dress, or another bride quite like that again."

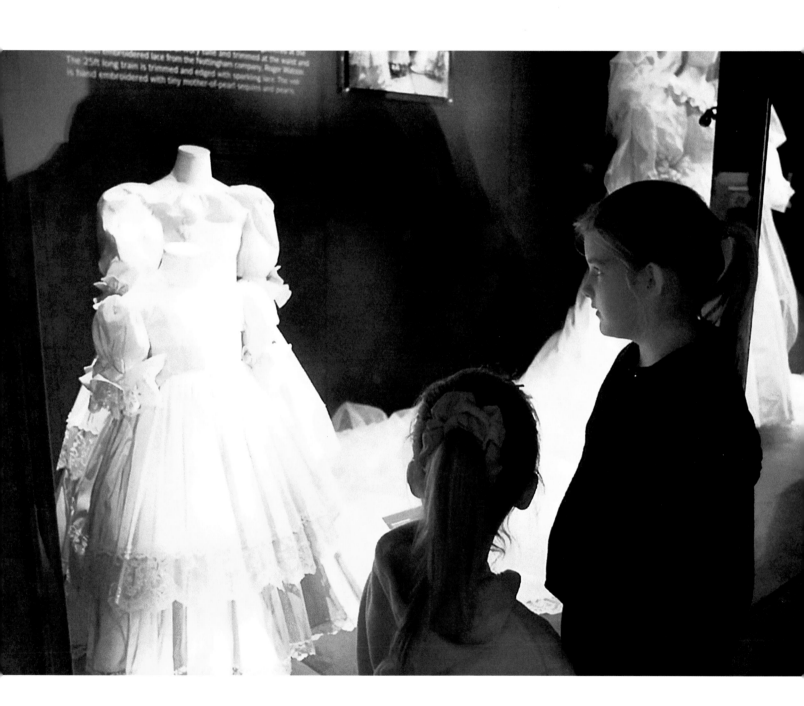

Above Since the Royal Wedding, where Princess Diana's dress was seen by an estimated 800 million via television networks world-wide, the gown has toured the world, giving millions more people the opportunity to view it. It now forms part of the permanent exhibition about Diana at the Spencer ancestral home at Althorp.

AUTHORS' ACKNOWLEDGEMENTS

Janet Fitzgerald – for her endless patience and hard work in the massive task of archiving the entire Royal Wedding collection.

Austin Shaw for his tremendous enthusiasm, vision and hard work in helping us to realize this book.

The Art of Being team – Kateryna Adamenko-Smith, Marina Gafurova, Samantha Cousins and Julia Ward for the many hours spent pressing and preparing the items for photography.

Richard Thompson for his encouragement and advice.

Michael Wicks for the most beautiful photographs.

My brother Charles Weiner and his wife Adele for always being there for me (from Liz).

Our children Oliver and Eloise who we are so proud of and who have been so supportive throughout the project.

To Beatrix Miller, Anna Harvey and Felicity Clark, who had faith in us from the very beginning.

Susanne Smith for her invaluable support "behind the scenes". Thank you (from David).

Finally, thank you to all the team at Pavilion, especially Kate Oldfield, Lizzy Gray, Louise Leffler and Anne McDowall, without whose immense effort we would not have been able to pull the book together.

For more information about Elizabeth Emanuel see her website at http://www.elizabethemanuel.co.uk contact: info@elizabethemanuel.co.uk

For more information about David Emanuel log onto: www.davidemanuel.com

Anova Books is committed to respecting the intellectual property rights of others. We have therefore taken all reasonable efforts to ensure that the reproduction of all content on these pages is done with the full consent of copyright owners. If you are aware of any unintentional omissions please contact the company directly so that any necessary corrections may be made for future editions.

UK & COMMONWEALTH FRONT JACKET: Fox Photos/ Getty Images; backcover: Peppermint Pictures Limited/photography by Michael Wicks; illustrations c. Elizabeth Emanuel; Author photos: right Peppermint Pictures Limited/Michael Wicks; left David Manton of Photodrome.

USA & CANADA FRONT JACKET: ©Quadrillion/CORBIS; backcover: Elizabeth Emanuel; Author photos: right Peppermint Pictures Limited/Michael Wicks; left David Manton of Photodrome.

1 Peppermint Picture Limited/photography by Michael Wicks; 2-3 ©Quadrillion/CORBIS; 4-5 Peppermint Pictures Limited/photography by Michael Wicks; 6-7 Patrick Lichfield/Camera Press London; 8 John Swannell; 12 Peppermint Pictures Limited/photography by Michael Wicks; 14 David Emanuel and Elizabeth Emanuel; 18 David Emanuel and Elizabeth Emanuel; 19 David Emanuel and Elizabeth Emanuel; 21 Private Collection; 25L Richard Young/Rex Features; 25R Tim Graham/Getty Images; 27 Snowdon/Camera Press London; 28 Peppermint Pictures Limited/photography by Michael Wicks 29 Peppermint Pictures Limited/photography by Michael Wicks; 30 David Emanuel and Elizabeth Emanuel; 31 Elizabeth Emanuel; 32 Alpha Press; 35 Richard Young/Rex Features; 37 David Emanuel and Elizabeth Emanuel; 38 Elizabeth Emanuel; 41 David Emanuel and Elizabeth Emanuel; 42 Private Collection; 46-47 David Emanuel and Elizabeth Emanuel; 50-51 David Emanuel and Elizabeth Emanuel; 53 Peppermint Picture Limited/photography by Michael Wicks 55L The Illustrated London News Picture Library/The Bridgeman Art Library; 55R Reproduction by kind permission of His Grace the Duke of Bedford and the Trustees of the Bedford Estates; 56-58, 60-61 David Emanuel and Elizabeth Emanuel; 59 Elizabeth Emanuel; 62-63 David Emanuel and Elizabeth Emanuel; 65 Tim Graham/Getty Images; 66 Peppermint Pictures Limited/photography by Michael Wicks 68 David Emanuel and Elizabeth Emanuel; 70-71 Rex Features; 73-75 David Emanuel and Elizabeth Emanuel; 76-83 Peppermint Pictures Limited/photography by Michael Wicks; 87-91 Peppermint Pictures Limited/photography by Michael Wicks; 92-97 David Emanuel and Elizabeth Emanuel; 98-99 Peppermint Pictures Limited/photography by Michel Wicks; 103 David Emanuel and Elizabeth Emanuel; 106-107 David Emanuel and Elizabeth Emanuel; 108-113 David Emanuel and Elizabeth Emanuel; 114 Peppermint Pictures Limited; 117 Private collection 118-119 Peppermint Pictures Limited/Photography by Michael Wicks; 120 Mike Edwards; 121-127 Clive Shilton & Julie Smith/photography by Theo Bergstrom; 128 Peppermint Pictures Limited/Photography by Michael Wicks; 129 David Emanuel and Elizabeth Emanuel; 130 Peppermint Pictures Limited/photography by Michael Wicks; 130-131 Longmans Limited/photography by Roger Scruton; 134R Peter Beales Roses; 134-135 Longmans Limited/photography by Roger Scruton; 136-139 Peppermint Pictures Limited/photography by Michael Wicks 141 Hulton Archive/Getty Images; 142-143 Peppermint Pictures Limited/photography by Michael Wicks; 145 Peppermint Pictures Limited/photography by Michael Wicks; 146-147 David Emanuel and Elizabeth Emanuel; 150-151 David Emanuel and Elizabeth Emanuel; 152-153 ©Popperfoto/Alamy; 155 David Emanuel and Elizabeth Emanuel; 157 David Emanuel and Elizabeth Emanuel; 159-161 © 2003 Arts and Exhibitions International LLC with permission from Althorp; 162L Peppermint Pictures Limited; 162 David Emanuel and Elizabeth Emanuel; 163 David Emanuel and Elizabeth Emanuel; 165-167 David Emanuel and Elizabeth Emanuel; 168 Empics; 170 David Emanuel and Elizabeth Emanuel; 171-4 Peppermint Pictures Limited/photography by Michael Wicks; 178 Peppermint Pictures Limited/photography by Michael Wicks; 181 Rex Features; 183L&R Rex Features; 184-185 ©Quadrillion/CORBIS; 186-187 Tim Graham/Getty Images; 188-189 ©Quadrillion/CORBIS; 191 Private Collection; 195 David Emanuel and Elizabeth Emanuel; 197-199 Reproduced with kind permission of Lady Sarah McCorquodale; 201 Reproduced with kind permission of Lord Fermoy; 205 Empics.

A DRESS FOR DIANA

HarperCollins books may be purchased for educational,
business, or sales promotional use. For information, please
write: Special Markets Department, HarperCollins
Publishers, 10 East 53rd Street, New York, NY 10022.

First Edition

First published in North America in 2006 by:
Collins Design
An Imprint of HarperCollins*Publishers*
10 East 53rd Street
New York, NY 10022
Tel: (212) 207-7000
Fax: (212) 207-7654
collinsdesign@harpercollins.com
www.harpercollins.com

Distributed throughout North America by:
HarperCollins*Publishers*
10 East 53rd Street
New York, NY 10022
Fax: (212) 207-7654

Library of Congress Control Number: 2006928281

ISBN-10: 0-06-121437-X
ISBN-13: 978-0-06-121437-0

Printed in the United Kingdom by Butler and Tanner
First printing, 2006